VOLUME 5

THE JOKER'S LAST LAUGH

HARLEY QUINN

HARLEY QUINN

VOLUME 5
THE JOKER'S LAST LAUGH

WRITTEN BY
AMANDA CONNER
JIMMY PALMIOTTI

ART BY
CHAD HARDIN
AMANDA CONNER

COLOR BY
ALEX SINCLAIR
PAUL MOUNTS

LETTERS BY
TOM NAPOLITANO
JOHN J. HILL

COLLECTION COVER ART BY
AMANDA CONNER
& ALEX SINCLAIR

HARLEY QUINN CREATED BY
PAUL DINI & BRUCE TIMM

CHRIS CONROY Editor - Original Series
DAVE WIELGOSZ Assistant Editor - Original Series
JEB WOODARD Group Editor - Collected Editions
ROBIN WILDMAN Editor - Collected Edition
STEVE COOK Design Director - Books
DAMIAN RYLAND Publication Design

HARLEY QUINN VOLUME 5: THE JOKER'S LAST LAUGH

DC Comics, 2900 West Alameda Ave., Burbank, CA 91505
Printed by RR Donnelley, Salem, VA, USA. 8/12/16. First Printing.
ISBN: 978-1-4012-6928-9

Library of Congress Cataloging-in-Publication Data is available.

BEVERLY HILLS.
HOW DO I *LOOK?*
TASTY.
I'LL *TAKE* IT. PUT IT ALL ON MY HUBBY'S CHARGE CARD.
YOU GOT IT, MRS. LAWTON. YOU NEED THE TOTAL?
LET'S KEEP IT A SURPRISE. FLOYD *ENJOYS* SURPRISES.
CUCCI

OF BEVERLY HILL
WINKIES BEVERLY HILLS
LAX, PLEASE. GOTTA PLANE TA CATCH, SO BOOGIE-WOOGIE.
YOU GOT IT!
LOCAL OR VISITING?
VISITIN'. I HAD ENOUGH.
IT'LL BE NICE TA HEAD BACK TA BROOKLYN WHERE PEOPLE TELL YA THEY HATE YA RIGHT TO YER FACE.
SPEAKING OF BROOKLYN...
WHO WANTS TO PICK UP OUR LOVELY LANDLORD AT THE AIRPORT?
UH... I JUST REMEMBERED... I NEED TO CLEAN UP AFTER THE ANIMALS UPSTAIRS.
I DON'T HAVE A DRIVER'S LICENSE.
DON'T LOOK AT ME.
I'LL DO IT!

DON'T EAT THESE. THEY AREN'T FOOD.
VERY FUNNY. LIKE I WOULD EAT CAR KEYS...
...AGAIN...
...AFTER THE HEARTBURN I HAD LAST TIME.
BRING HER STRAIGHT BACK, GOATBOY. NO SIDE TRIPS TO BURGER CASTLE OR WIENER KING.

NO PROBLEM, BIG TONY. I'LL GET HER BACK ZIPPIDY-DOO!

UNDISCLOSED LOCATION ON
E NORTH SHORE SECTION OF LONG ISLAND,
E WEEK AGO.
ERIK, TIME FOR BREAKFAST. FRIED EGGS VIT KIELBASA ENT DEELL TOPPINK.

WHAT TIME IS IT?
10:30.
THERE IS BELL RINGING IN BASEMENT FOR HOUR NOW. I WOULD SHUT IT, BUT YOU SAID NO ENTRY.
AN HOUR? BAD GIRL. YOU WERE SUPPOSED TO WAKE ME.

USUAL DISCIPLINE? I HAFF UNIFORM IN OTHER ROOM. I GET IT, AND SADDLE, TOO.
RAIN CHECK, VALERIYA. I HAVE WORK TO DO.

BUT...ZIS BREAKFAST!
EAT IT YOURSELF. CLOSE THAT DOOR AND NO CALLS TILL I'M DONE. PONIMAYETE?
YA. UNDERSTOOD.

BEEP! BEEP! BEEP!
YES, YES, I'M COMING.
MY BABUSHKA WILL BE SO PROUD OF ME!
FINALLY!
BLOOD PRESSURE'S WITHIN RANGE...
...ARTERIES ALL CLEAR...
...BLOOD FLOW TO ALL POINTS OF THE BODY IS.. SEAMLESS.
EVEN THOUGH I HAD TO REFABRICATE 74% OF YOUR BODY, THE MOST IMPORTANT PARTS WERE SAVED AND IMPROVED BY YOUR LOVING GRANDSON, BABUSHKA!
AFTER ALL YOUR MINI-STROKES, ANEURISMS AND HORRIBLY BAD CHOLESTEROL, WELL...THE NEW HEART I BUILT FOR YOU WILL GIVE YOU THE ENERGY OF AN ANGRY TEENAGE EX-GIRLFRIEND!
WHEN I PRESS THIS BUTTON, YOU WILL BE ALIVE ONCE MORE TO UNLEASH YOUR FURY ONTO THE WORLD!
Hmmm, MAYBE THIS ISN'T SUCH A GOOD IDEA.
SHE WOULDN'T BE MAD AT ME, RIGHT?
I MEAN, SY BORGMAN'S THE ONE RESPONSIBLE FOR HER HORRIBLE DEATH BY RHINO HORN.*
I'M THE ONE BRINGING HER BACK.
SHE MIGHT EVEN THINK THE WORLD OF ME AND MAKE ME PART OF HER CRIME ORGANIZATION. THAT WOULD BE VERY COOL...
...AS LONG AS SHE'S OKAY WITH ME SPENDING MOST OF HER FORTUNE ON THIS EXPERIMENT.
*See HARLEY QUINN VOL. 1: HOT IN THE CITY
Ah WELL...
...HERE GOES NOTHING.
ZZZOTT
WHOAAAAA

IT WORKED! GRANDMA! I SAVED YOU!
DO YOU FEEL ALL RIGHT? CAN YOU SPEAK?
IS THERE ANYTHING YOU WANT TO TELL ME?
SY BORGMAN AND HARLEY QUINN MUST DIE!!!
AMANDA CONNER & JIMMY PALMIOTTI WRITERS
CHAD HARDIN ARTIST
ALEX SINCLAIR COLORS TOM NAPOLITANO LETTERS
AMANDA CONNER & ALEX SINCLAIR COVER
CHAD HARDIN & ALEX SINCLAIR VARIANT COVER
AMANDA CONNER, PAUL MOUNTS & SPIKE BRANDT LOONEY TUNES VARIANT COVER
DAVE WIELGOSZ ASST. EDITOR CHRIS CONROY EDITOR
MARK DOYLE GROUP EDITOR
HARLEY QUINN CREATED BY PAUL DINI & BRUCE TIMM

KENNEDY AIRPORT, RIGHT NOW.
Ahh. HOLEE HOME-SWEET-FRIGGIN'-HOME. I SURE MISS BROOKLYN.
THIS IS QUEENS.
YOU SEE EVERYTHING, DON'CHA?
MY BUDDIES ARE SENDIN' A CAR FOR ME... WHAT ABOUT YOU?
SON'S COMING HERE TO GET ME. NICE OF YOU TO CHAT WITH ME THE WHOLE WAYS BACK FROM LOS ANGELES. HOPE I WASN'T A PEST.
AW, DON'T BE SILLY.
Gates
ALL A' YER INSIGHT INTA WHAT BEIN' BLIND IS LIKE'LL HELP ME RELATE TA ONE A' MY WORKERS BETTER. Y'GOT MY NUMBER NOW AND I'M A PHONE CALL AWAY.
DAD!
TIMMY!
AWWWWWW. I'M ALL MELTY INSIDE.
YOU MEET A MOVIE STAR ON THE PLANE, YOU OLD DOG?
TIMMY, THIS IS HARLEY. SHE LIVES IN CONEY. SHE KEPT ME COMPANY THE WHOLE WAY ACROSS THE COUNTRY.
IT'S THE OTHER WAY AROUND. YOUR DAD'S THE BEST.
WELL, IT'S NICE TO MEET YOU. NEED A LIFT HOME? WE'RE PASSING THAT WAY...
"AW, THANKS, BUT I GOT SOMEONE PICKIN' ME UP."

CAPITALIST SWINE QUINN
WELL, I SEE MY RIDE.
TAKE *CARE* OF EACH OTHER!

THAT'S *ME, GODZILLA.* WHATTA THEY *FEEDIN'* YOU AT HOME?
FOOD.
YOU HAFF BAGS?
JUST THE ONE I'M CARRYIN'. THIS *FOOD* YA EAT... DOES IT GROW NEAR *THREE MILE ISLAND?*
WE *GO* NOW.

THEY MUSTA REALLY MISSED ME, GOIN' TA ALL THIS TROUBLE. TONY SENT YA, RIGHT?
SURE. TONY.
WHAT'S YER HANDLE?
YURY. YOU GO INSIDE NOW.

DO ME A FAVOR AN' *TAKE* YER *TIME* GETTING ME HOME...I'M GONNA *ENJOY* THIS.
THERE A *SHOWER* IN HERE?

HEY YO-YO, HOW ABOUT *SAMMICHES?*
IN COOLER BY ICE. ENJOY FINAL MEAL.
Huh? WHUZZAT?
VEAL. I ONLY ENJOY FINE VEAL.

WE MAKIN' A *PIT STOP?*
YES, PICKINK UP FRIENDS.

YOURS OR *MINE?*

MINE.

PERFORATION TIME, TOVARISHCHI.
BLAM BLAM
BLAM
BLAM
BLAM

WOW, SOMEONE REALLY HATES LIMOUSINES. I BET IT HAS SOMETHIN' TA DO WITH A MISSED PROM. AT LEAST THEY'RE CONSIDERATE AN' NOT SHOOTIN' YOUR SECTION, eh, YOGI?
BLAM
BLAM BLAM
HEY, KING KONG, Y'GOT ANY FIREPOWER ON YOU?
ughhhhh
DON'T SWEAT IT, I'LL FEEL AROUND.
BLAM BLAM BLAM

WELL, THAT'S NOT A GUN, BUT YOU COULD SURE HURT SOMEONE WITH THAT!
Ah HA... BINGO!
BLAMBLAMBLAMBLAM
BLAMBLAMBLAMBLAMBLAM

SOMESING IS WRONG.
YURY! DEED WE GET HER?

NO, PRINCESS. NICE TRY, THOUGH.
BLAM!

GAHHH!
BLAM BLAM BLAM BLAM
BLAM BLAM BLAM BLAM BLAM BLAM BLAM BLAM
BLAM
BLAM
BLAM BLAM BLAM
BLAM BLAM
BLAM BLAM
BLAM BLAM
BOY, I MUSTA *REALLY* PISSED SOMEONE OFF.
I TAKE NO CHANCES.
FOOOSH
KA-BOOM
YIKES! NO FAIR!

CLICK
CLICK
WHAT THE... IZZIS SOME KINDA RUSSIAN ROULETTE JOKE? ONLY ONE BULLET?

OUTGUNNED. GOTTA MUSTER UP SOME MUNITIONS.

Hmmm, OFFICE SUPPLIES.
MUST MACGYVER MYSELF SOMETHIN' LICKETY-SPLIT.

I TEENK WE GOT HER. IT'S WERY QUIET.
MAKE SURE JOB IS DONE, OTHERWISE WE ARE.

NO SUCH LUCK, HOTTIES! CATCH THIS...

AGGGHHH! MY EYE!

TELL ME WHAT THIS IS ABOUT AN' I'LL GET AN AMBULANCE HERE PDQ.
SENT... TO KEEL YOU...
NO KIDDIN', KARENINA. I WANNA KNOW WHO AN' WHY. YOU LOOK AN' SOUND LIKE A FRIEND OF AN ENEMY OF A FRIEND A' MINE, BUT SHE'S DEAD FROM THE BUSINESS END OF A RHINO.
EET... EET IS HER...
ZENA BENDEMOVA?
NO WAY. SHE LEAVE ORDERS IN HER WILL OR SOMETHIN'?
THAT'S COMMITMENT.
WELL, YA DID TELL ME, SO I'M CALLIN' 9-1-1. HANG IN THERE...
9-1-1... WHAT IS YOUR EMERGENCY?
HCCCCH
Uh-oh. HOLEE TERMINOLEE, NEVER MIND.

ROAD WORK AHEAD
ARCADE
YES, I'LL ACCEPT THE CHARGES.
CONEY ISLAND.
MADAME MACABRE'S HOUSE OF WAX AND MURDER.
MASON...YOU THERE?
MASON? HELLO?
"OUT OF IT."
MOM, YOU GOTTA GET ME OUTTA HERE.
I GOT INMATES AND GUARDS GUNNING FOR ME. SOMEONE PUT A HIT ON ME, MA.
THEY WON'T EVEN PUT ME IN SOLITARY... THEY PATCH ME UP AND RELEASE ME BACK INTO GENERAL POPULATION EVERY TIME.
HOW CAN THEY DO THIS TO YOU! YOU'RE SUPPOSED TO BE PROTECTED IN THERE!
IT'S HELL, MOM. I DUNNO WHAT TO DO...
YOU FIGHT FOR YOUR LIFE! THAT'S WHAT YOU DO!
I AM, BUT I'M PRETTY OUTNUMBERED.
TIME'S UP, SKIPPER.
HEY! I'M ON THE PHONE.
NOT ANYMORE.

WHUMPP

NCHHH

MASON!
MASON!!
"OUT OF IT!"
IN THE POLITE COMIC PLAY

WHOP

WHAKK

YOU... YOU...

...MISERABLE...

...LITTLE...

...RAT TÜRDS!
AAAAHHHGGH
KRAKK

WHUMPP

KONKK

YOU HEAR A *SCREAM?*
MAYBE SOMEONE'S GETTIN' LUCKY?
SOUNDED LIKE *MADAME MACABRE.* WE OUGHTA CHECK IT OUT.

MASON!
BAFF

TZZZZZZZZZZT
GAAAHHHHH!

GOOD BOY. STAY DOWN.
RAMONE, TAKE ALL THREE OF THESE MEN TO THE INFIRMARY.
MASON!

MASON, WHAT'S HAPPENING?!?

AN' TO WHOM AM I SPEAKIN'?
MY SON, IS HE ALL RIGHT?

CLICK!
HE'S AS GOOD AS DEAD, LADY.

Yawwwwnnnn!
G'MORNIN', MIKE, BERNIE. HOW ARE MY SWEETIES DOIN'?
IT'S AFTERNOON, YA WOOD SAWIN' WACKO.
RIGHT. WELL, THANK GOD I TOOK TODAY OFF. I'M HUNGRY.
I WANT PANCAKES!
HEY, ANY CHANCE YA CAN LAY SOME PANCAKES FER MOMMY?
FIRST, MIKE IS A ROOSTER, NOT A HEN.
SECOND, YOU DIDN'T GIVE BIRTH TO HIM, SO STOP CALLIN' YOURSELF MOMMY.
IT'S JUST DISTURBIN'.
Hmmph. SOUNDS LIKE SOMEBODY WOKE UP ON THE WRONG SIDE OF THE DAM!
I MUST LET THE WORLD KNOW ABOUT MY CRAVING.
I WANT PANCAKES AND I WANT THEM NOW!
NOBODY CARES! SHUT YOUR GIANT PANCAKE HOLE AND GET YER ASS BACK TA THE KITCHEN, NUTMUFFIN!
HAHA HAHA
WELL, I NEVER...
STICKS AN' STONES MAY HURT MY BONES, BUT THIS IS GONNA HURT A LOT MORE!
YA WANT ME TO BUILD A BELL TOWER FOR YOU WHILE WE'RE AT IT?
NO TIME. I GOTTA TEACH THESE CAVE DWELLERS SOME MANNERS.

JUST A TINY LI'L ADJUSTMENT AN'...
...huh?

REALLY?
NOW?

IS THE UNIVERSE TRYIN' TA TELL ME SOMETHIN'?
Aw, HOW'S MOMMA'S LITTLE FLYIN' MONKEYS DOIN'? DIDJA MISS ME?
TWEET TWEET

YES! I DID MISS YOU!!!
TWEET TWEET TWEET

Hmm... JUST HOW SMART ARE YOU FEATHERY LI'L FUSSBUDGIES?
CAN YOU LITTLE DARLINGS DO MOMMA A BIG FAVOR?

Huh?
THAT A GREEN CLOUD?

FAP FAP
FAP FAP
FAPPITY
FAP FAP
SHLAP
SHLAP
SHLAP
SPLAP
PLAP
AAAAGGGGHH!

HEY TONY, I SAW GOATBOY ON THE WAY DOWNSTAIRS. HE TOLD ME ABOUT HIS INVOLUNTARY SLUMBER PARTY WITH THE CLEANIN' SUPPLIES AT THE AIRPORT.
THANKS AGAIN FOR PICKIN' ME UP LAST NIGHT.
PEACHES! I'M GLAD YOU'RE UP--
I KNOW...I GOTTA TELL SY ABOUT ZENA PUTTIN' A HIT ON US...
...BUT BREAKFAST FIRST! I'M STARVIN', AN' IT'S BETTER TO FOREWARN ON A FULL TUMMY.

WANNA JOIN ME? AFTER LAST NIGHT'S ANTISOCIAL ANTICS, I'M CRAVIN' SOME MAJOR JOHNNYCAKES.
I WANT ONES WITH CHOCOLATE AN' BLUEBERRIES IN 'EM, AN' LOTTSA SYRUP... A TREE'S WORTH. OH, AN' A BARREL A' COFFEE TA TOP IT OFF.

HEY, WHY SO QUIET? THAT'S NOT LIKE YOU.
I WAS WAITIN' 'TIL YA CAME UP FER AIR.
IT'S MASON... HE GOT BEAT UP AGAIN, PRETTY BADLY.

AGAIN? WHAT THE...?
HE'S CONVINCED THERE'S A HIT ON HIM, AN' HE'S FIGHTIN' FER HIS LIFE.
HE'S TAKEN A FEW BEATINGS THIS PAST WEEK... AN' IT DOESN'T LOOK LIKE IT'S GONNA GET ANY BETTER.
WHY? I MEAN, WHO...

HARLEY, HE'S ACCUSED OF KILLIN' THE MAYOR'S SON. COULD BE THE MAYOR OR ANY NUMBER A' PEOPLE TRYIN' TA WIN HIS FAVOR.
BOTTOM LINE IS, HE'S GOOD AS DEAD IF HE STAYS THERE. MADAME MACABRE IS TALKIN' TA THE LAWYERS RIGHT NOW.

I GOTTA OPEN FER THE AFTERNOON SHOW. DO ME A FAVOR AN' CALL SY ABOUT LAST NIGHT FIRST... THEN YA CAN EAT YERSELF INTO A STUPOR.
FERGET IT. I JUST LOST MY APPETITE.

NO, *NO SIGN* OF HIM, DR. QUINZEL. THE POLICE SEARCHED THE BUILDING AND *NOTHING.*
HIS ROOM LOOKS LIKE *WORLD WAR THREE* TOOK PLACE.
NO BLOOD, THOUGH.
POLICE LINE DO NOT CROSS POLICE LINE DO NOT CROSS
NYPD

DO ME A FAVOR, *SAKIM*... JUST *CALL ME* IF YOU HEAR *ANYTHING!*
NO MATTER WHAT TIME, *DAY* OR *NIGHT.* THANKS.

COACH!
RALLY THE TROOPS AN' HAVE 'EM MEET ME IN THE BASEMENT, *PRONTO!*

NOT THAT I DON'T APPRECIATE THE CLOTHES-FREE CAVALCADE AS MUCH AS THE *NEXT* GIRL, BUT DID THE BUNCH A' YOU *JUST WAKE UP?*
WE JUST FINISHED AN OVERNIGHT GIG THAT INVOLVED A GROUP OF HOODS SHAKING DOWN SOME LOCAL BAKERIES.
WE MADE ABOUT *TWELVE GRAND* ON THE GIG AND ALL THE *CRUMB CAKE* WE CAN EAT FOR LIFE. EVERYONE WAS RESTING UP.
Oooh, CRUMB CAKE FER... *HEY--!*
CENSORED

HARLEM HARLEY, WHAT'S THAT UNDER YER ARM?
IT'S MY BEDTIME BINKY.
MY OLD BOYFRIEND GAVE IT TO ME. WHY?

I-I KNOW THAT...GUY. IT'S JUST SO WEIRD SEEING HIM USED AS A SECURITY ANYTHING.
CAN I SEE THAT?

THIS...TOYBOY...TORMENTED THE HELL OUTTA ME. IT'S SO FREAKY SEEIN' HIM BEIN' REPRESENTED THIS WAY.
HE...THE CRAP HE DID TA ME...SOMETIMES GOOD, MOSTLY BAD...
WAIT...I DON'T GET IT...IT'S A TOY.

USING THE DOLL, SHOW US WHERE HE TOUCHED YOU.
REALLY? YOU HADDA GO THERE?

HE TOUCHED ME HERE...
RIPPPPP

...IN MY HEAD!
RIPPP!!

YA HAPPY NOW?

I... uh...
SORRY.
YIKES.
IT'S OKAY! I FEEL BETTER NOW!

SOOO... HARLEY QUEENS, WHY ARE YOU TOPLESS?

NUMBER ONE, JUST LOOK AT THESE!
NUMBER TWO,...WELL, JUST LOOK AT 'EM!
CENSORED

THOSE ARE TWO GOOD POINTS. CHANGE A' SUBJECT.

I GOT A GIG. IT'S A PERSONAL FAVOR. FEEL FREE TA PASS ON IT IF YOU LIKE. I WILL NOT HOLD IT AGAINST YOU.
MY GOOD FRIEND WAS ACCUSED A' MURDER AN' HE'S DOIN' TIME UPSTATE. HE'S FIGHTIN' FER HIS LIFE.
I'M GONNA HELP HIM AN' I'M LOOKIN' FER VOLUNTEERS TA GIMME A HAND BUSTIN' HIM OUT.

I'M IN. I CAN STAY HERE AND MONITOR THE OPERATION.

I KNOW MY WAY AROUND A MEN'S PRISON BETTER THAN ANYONE. COUNT ME IN.

SOUNDS LIKE A CHALLENGE.

I GOTTA PASS.
IT'S MY SECOND COUSIN'S BAR MITZVAH THIS WEEKEND. IF I BAIL, A LOT OF OLD PEOPLE LOSE THEIR RIDE, INCLUDING YOUR BUDDY SY.
Oh CRAP! IT TOTALLY SLIPPED MY MIND!

HANNAH, SOMEONE RAIDED YOUR GREAT UNCLE'S ROOM AT THE HOME, AN' HE'S MISSIN'.
COACH, GET ME THE NAMES AND ADDRESSES TO ANYONE CONNECTED TO ZENA BENDEMOVA.
SOME A' ZENA'S FLUNKY FLOOZIES TRIED TA VENTILATE ME LAST NIGHT. SOMEBODY WANTS TA GET REVENGE ON ME AN' SY FER DECEASIFYIN' HER.
SERIOUSLY, IT WASN'T ME, IT WAS THE RHINO HORN THAT KILLED HER.

WHY ARE WE STANDING HERE WITH OUR YOGURT SLINGERS IN OUR HANDS? WE HAVE TO FIND UNCLE SY!
WHATNOW?
OH. RIGHT. WE SPLIT UP. HARVEY QUINN, HARLEM HARLEY AND HARLEY QUEENS, COME WITH ME.
COACH, YOU AN' THE REST FOLLOW ANY LEADS YOU CAN FIND. IF WE LEAVE TONIGHT, WE CAN FREE MASON AN' BE BACK TOMORROW.

WELL, JUST DON'T STAND THERE TWIDDLIN' YER CHOCOLATE DONUTS!
GET DRESSED AND READY TA KICK SOME ASS.
THIS POOP'S GETTIN' REAL!

NOT NEW JERSEY.
Huh. I DUNNO WHO THIS IS CALLIN' ME.
IS IT A TELEMARKETER? LET'S SCREW WITH 'EM!

'ELLO, MISERABLE CREEPY LEETLE POOP STAIN OF EENSECT.

YER GONNA HAVETA BE MORE SPECIFIC ABOUT WHO THIS IS.
I'M COUNTIN' AT LEAST A DOZEN DIFFERENT INDIVIDUALS WHO WOULD TALK TA ME LIKE THAT.
HOWS 'BOUT A HINT?

MAYBE ZEES WILL GIFF YOU CLUE!

OWWW! MAY YOU FALL INTO AN OUTHOUSE JUST AS A REGIMENT OF UKRAINIANS ARE FINISHING PRUNE STEW AND TWELVE BARRELS OF BEER!
SY BORGMAN!
WAITAMINIT...

...IS THIS ZENA BENDEMOVA?
ZE ONE ENT ONLY!
MEES ME?

I MISS YOU LIKE I MISS HERPES!
YOU TOUCH ONE A' THE SEVENTEEN HAIRS ON HIS HEAD AN' I'LL KILL YOU AGAIN!
YOU VANT HEEM SO BADLY? COME GET HEEM. VE ARE AT ISLAND LANES ON FLATBOOSH. I LEAVE FRONT DOOR OPEN.
I'M...UH... IN JERSEY, SO GIMME AN HOUR.
YOU KNOW HOW THE BRIDGE IS THIS TIME A' DAY.

AT LEAST THEY HEET YOU UP FOR TOLL ONLY GOING VON VAY. ZE OLD VAY HAFF DELAYS ON BOTH ENDS.
YEAH, BUT IT'S LIKE TWENNY-FIVE BUCKS NOW. THEY OUGHTA GIVE YOU A MASSAGE WITH THAT, Y'KNOW?

I MEAN, I CAN ALMOST BUY FIVE COMICS WITH THAT. IT'S CRIME ON A WEDNESDAY, I TELL YA.
SO YEAH, ONE HOUR. GET READY TA GETCHER HOARY WRINKLED BUTT BOOTED BY YOURS TRULY.
CHANGE A' PLANS, EVERYBODY. MASON HAS TA WAIT.
I GOTTA MATCHPLAY SIX PACK ON OLD ENEMY A FRIEND.
HANUQUINN, YOU COME WITH ME SINCE IT'S YER UNCLE I'M SAVIN'. EVERYONE STAY PUT 'TIL WE GET BACK.

HOW DO I LOOK?
WAIT... WE STOPPED SO YOU COULD CHANGE YOUR COSTUME?!
Shh... DON'T.
BRUNSWICK BABES
KINGPIN QUEEN
AMANDA CONNER & JIMMY PALMIOTTI WRITERS
CHAD HARDIN ARTIST
ALEX SINCLAIR COLORS TOM NAPOLITANO LETTERS
AMANDA CONNER & ALEX SINCLAIR COVER & 1:25 VARIANT COVER
BRUCE TIMM BLACK BOOK VARIANT COVER
DAVE WIELGOSZ ASST. EDITOR CHRIS CONROY EDITOR
MARK DOYLE GROUP EDITOR
HARLEY QUINN CREATED BY PAUL DINI & BRUCE TIMM

IT'S WHY I TOLD 'ER I WAS IN JERSEY. I LIKE THE OUTFIT TA FIT THE OCCASION, PLUS IT GIVES ME TIME TA WORK OUT THE DETAILS A' THE PLAN.
SO YOU HAVE A PLAN?
AW, THIS SHOULD BE GOOD.
OR NOT.
MY PLAN IS TA VENNILATE THE OL' LADY AN' THEN TAKE SY OUT FER A NICE PASTRAMI SAMMICH.
I HAVE NO IDEA HOW SHE'S ALIVE, BUT SHE'S LIKE, A MILLION YEARS OLD, SO HOW HARD COULD IT BE?
Y'KNOW HOW TA USE THIS?

YES, BUT I'LL DO MY BEST NOT TO KILL ANYONE.
SHKK-CHKK
AW, GOOD INTENTIONS. I ADMIRE THAT.
SADLY, THIS SADISTIC BITCH ALREADY TRIED TA KILL ME, SO THE DAMAGE IS DONE.
SHKK-CHKK
LET'S HOPE YER LOVELY UNCLE SY IS STILL KICKIN'.

SO, DO WE JUST BUST ROUGH THE FRONT OOR AND START SHOOTING?
Island Lanes BOWLING
I'M THINKIN' SHE'LL BE WAITIN'. LET'S TAKE A QUICK PEEK-A-BOO.
ghhh, MAYBE IF U PUT THE GUN WN, THIS MIGHT BE EASIER.
NOT POSSIBLE. PUSH HARDER.
-I'M...ugh... TRYING...
IS IT WRONG THAT I'M ENJOYIN' THIS?
LITTLE... FURTHER...
GOOD. I CAN SEE--
Oh NO... THIS IS WORSE THAN I THOUGHT.
QUICK, LEMME DOWN.

Jm... LET'S EAD HOME. NOW.
SERIOUSLY.
THIS CASE JUST SOLVED ITSELF.
WHAT DO YOU MEAN? IS MY UNCLE SY DEAD?!?

I THOUGHT SO--WELL, FROM THE WAIST DOWN ANYWAY, BUT I WAS JUST PROVEN WRONG.
I'LL NEVER BE ABLE TO UN-SEE WHAT I JUST SAW FER THE REST A' MY LIFE.

I HAVE TO SEE THIS FOR MYSELF.
NO. NO. NO YOU DON'T.

HOLEE FOSSILY SAUSAGES...
OH MY GOD! UNCLE SY!!!
Yeesh. I WARNED HER. I REALLY DID.

WHY? WHY DIDN'T YOU WARN ME? WHAT IS WRONG WITH YOU???
ME?? I DID WARN YOU!
WELL... NOT HARD ENOUGH! I MAY NEVER EAT AGAIN!

EEYUNKES!

SY I FORGEEV, BUT YOU?...NOT SO MUCH!
-Gakkk-

WHOOOO!!!
WHAMSK!

KER-BAMDIT
!

YOU MAY BE HOOKING UP WITH MY UNCLE, BUT THAT'S MY BOSS YOU JUST BOWLED!
AH, SO YOU ARE HANNAH. SY SAID YOU VERE ZE BEAUTY.
VY YOU HANG AROUND VITH PSYCHO? YOU CAN DO SO MUCH BETTER FOR YOURSELF.
AND EET'S NOT POLITE TO POINT.
KRNNCH
-Eeep- SORRY.
I...WE THOUGHT SY WAS IN TROUBLE. I MEAN, WE THOUGHT YOU WERE SETTING US UP FOR...

I VAS... AN HOUR AGO I VOULD'VE KEELED ALL THREE OF YOU, BUT LOVE HAPPENED.
YOUR UNCLE AND I...VE HAFF HEESTORY.
IT VASN'T UNTIL I TORTURE HEEM ZAT WE COME TO ZE REALIZATION THERE EES FLAME NOT EVEN DEATH COULD EXTEENGUISH.

SURE, I TRY TO KEEL HEEM. HE DROVE ME INTO RHINO HORN AT ZOO AND KEEL ME, BUT ZAT'S ZE PAST.
MY VNUK BROUGHT ME BACK TO LIFE AND NOW I VANT TO CHANGE MY VAYS. SVITCH SIDES, BECOME HERO. NOT MUCH BETTER PAY THAN SOVIET KOMANDIR, BUT MORE PRAISES.
SO WHY ARE YOU STILL TRYING TO KILL HARLEY?
ZAT LOONY TOON ANNOYS ME. BE RIGHT BACK.

C'MON SY, SHOOT ONE A' YER GRENADE BAGELS AT 'ER--AN' IF Y'GOT A CINNAMON RAISIN IN THERE, I'M STARVIN'.
SHE WON'T HURT YOU.
GETTIN' MY PHARYNX FINGERED AN' MY ASS THROWN DOWN THE ALLEY TELLS ME OTHERWISE.
KISHKA, SHE'S MY LIBE. STOP KVETCHING.

HOW 'BOUT I JUST HURT HER LEETLE MORE, BUT NOT KEEL HER? WOULD ZAT BE OKAY, DARLEENK?
NO. YOU ALREADY OWE HER AN APOLOGY FOR SENDING YOUR CREW TO KILL HER. PLEASE, LIBE.
SY BORGMAN, YOU HAFF POWER OVER ME I CANNOT RESEEST.

THEN DON'T.
SMERPP

ZEES EES NICE. I HOPE MY GRANDSON PUT SOME KIND OF BACK DOOR EENTO MY NEW BIONIC BODY.
HE DID, AND YOUR TUCHES NEVER LOOKED BETTER, MY MALKE.
OH. PLEASE. NO.
ISN'T LOVE GRAND? SO NOW THAT YER A COUPLE, WHAT ARE YER PLANS?

MY GRANDSON VILL PEEK ME UP SOON, ZEN SY AND I MUST... WELL...
WHAT SHE'S TRYING TO SAY IS WE BOTH HAVE ENEMIES. WE'R TOGETHER NOW, SO BO SIDES'LL THINK WE'RE SHARING CLASSIFIED INFORMATION...
...WHEN THE ONLY SCHEMATIC I'M INTERESTED IN IS THE ONE THAT TELLS ME WHICH BUTTONS TO PRESS ON MY KHAVERTE RIGHT HERE

BEFORE YOUR IMAGINATION GOES VILD, I ACTUALLY HAVE MANY BUTTONS ON ME AND I HAFF NO IDEA WHAT ZEY ARE FOR.
uuurrp

SO YA FINK BOFE SIDES chomp ARE GONNA COME AFTER YOU GUYS?
SEND gulp HIT SQUADS AN' ALL THAT?

YES. THE PLAN IS TO HEAD TO THE BAHAMAS, TO ZENA'S PRIVATE VILLA, AND PICK THEM OFF ONE BY ONE AS THEY COME AFTER US. THAT WAY NO CIVILIANS GET HURT.
IT SHOULD TAKE A FEW MONTHS...BUT EVENTUALLY WE'LL BE ABLE TO COME BACK.

OOO. PICKIN' OFF PERPS IN PARADISE? CALL ME IF YOU NEED ANY HELP!
SURE, GENDSEL. DON'T YOU WORRY.
MEETING YOU VAS TOTAL PLEASURE.
DEED I TELL YOU MY GRANDSON EES SEENGLE?
Uhh...

UPSTATE NEW YORK. A FEW HOURS LATER.
I'M NOT USED TO SEEIN' YOU WITH SO MUCH CLOTHING, HARVEY.
H&B Clinton Correctional Facility
YEAH, I'VE BEEN DYING TO WEAR THIS SUIT FOR A WHILE. IT COST ME A FEW MONTHS' RENT, BUT THE CUT IS FABULOUS.
I FIGURED WHILE I'M HERE, I MIGHT RUN INTO A FEW OLD FRIENDS.
THE INFIRMARY'S AHEAD.
I HOPE MASON IS OKAY.
HELLO. DR. QUINZEL. I'M HERE TO SEE PRISONER 8675309.
MACABRE? HE'S BEEN CHECKED OUT AN' SENT BACK TO HIS CELL.
WELL, WE NEED TO SEE HIM. THE MAYOR'S OFFICE SENT ME TO SPEAK WITH HIM, AND UPDATE THEM ON HIS CONDITION.
THAT SO?
WHY DON'T I GIVE HIS OFFICE A CALL AN' CHECK ON THIS. WHAT D'YA THINK OF THAT?
I THINK YOU SHOULD STOP WASTING AIR AND MAKE THE CALL ALREADY.
WELL THEN, I THINK I WILL.
PLEASE, BEFORE I GET OLD AND DIE.
YES, MAY I SPEAK TO THE MAYOR? HE IS? WHO'S THIS?
FINE. I HAVE A DR. QUINZEL HERE WITH AN ASSISTANT SAYIN' SHE WAS SENT TO CHECK IN ON PRISONER MASON MACABRE?

YES, OUR OFFICE COMMISSIONED THE DOCTOR TO CHECK HIS CONDITION AND MAKE SURE HE HAS WHAT HE *NEEDS*. DO WE *UNDERSTAND* EACH OTHER?
I GOTCHA *LOUD* AN' *CLEAR*. THANKS.
THE PRISONERS ARE IN THE SHOWERS RIGHT NOW, SO YA MIGHT *NOT* BE *NEEDED*, IF YOU KNOW WHAT I *MEAN*, DOC.
YA SHOULDA JUST *TOLD* ME YOU WERE HIRED TO TAKE OUT THE MACABRE GUY *BEFORE* MAKIN' ME CALL THE MAYOR'S OFFICE.
YER *LAST CREW* DID SOME DAMAGE ON HIM, BUT NOT ENOUGH TO SEAL THE DEAL.
I AIN'T NEVER SEEN SUCH *PRETTY* HIRED KILLERS BEFORE.
ARE YOU TALKING TO *HER* OR *ME?*
REALLY, HARVEY?
BOTH A' YOU.
KONK
ALRIGHT, YOU. *NAPPY TIME.*

DON'T LET ANYONE IN. USE FORCE IF YOU HAVE TO. I'M GONNA GO GET MASON OUT OF HERE ONCE AN' FER ALL.
LOCK THE DOOR BEHIND ME AN' STAY IN CONTACT WITH HARLEY QUEENS. HAVE HER KEEP AN EYE OUT AS WELL.
JEEZ, I'M SWIMMIN' IN THIS MONKEY SUIT.
C'MERE, I GOTTA PACKAGE FOR YOU!
WOOO!
'EY TASTY LADY!
YOU LIKE FROSTED DONUTS, MAMA?
KEEP IT IN YER PANTS, PERPS...
I'MA EATCHOO UP, CLOWN CHOW!
...BEFORE I POUND ALL A' YER PATHETIC PRISON PATOOTIES!
Showers
BINGO!
BARE-ASSED BADDIES, HERE I COME!

THAT'S IT! STICK THE SON OF A BITCH GOOD!
WATCH HIS HANDS...HIT HIM HARDER!
I CAN'T BELIEVE MY TAX DOLLARS ARE GOIN' TO A BRICK-HEADED DOINK-NUT SUCH AS YERSELF.
Huh, WHO THE HELL ARE--

SHUT YER FLAPPIN' FACE-HOLE, YA SNIVELIN' SNOTBAG.
KRRNCH

GASP
PAYLOADS A' PUMMELIN'...
MASON!
HARLEY...?!?

?
Oh NO, ARE YOU OKAY?
DID THESE MEANIES HURT YOU??
NO.
A LITTLE BIT.
WELL LOOKEE HERE! HE CALLED IN CIRCUS SECURITY.
Haw! TODAY JUST KEEPS GETTIN' BETTER AN' BETTER!

WHATTA SPECIAL TREAT. I HAVEN'T KILLED A WOMAN SINCE I WAS PUT IN HERE TEN YEARS AGO.
Heh. FUN FIRST.
THEN SAY LATER MUCH TO LIVIN', SWEETIE.

TOUGH TALK FROM TURD-HOLES. YER GONNA MAKE THIS REAL FUN FER ME.
WHICH ONE A' YOU GUYS WANTS TA BE A POPSICLE FIRST?

FACE, MEET FOOT.
HOW D'YA DO, FACE!
KICKK
Ooof!
CRANIUM, MEET CLUB.
WELL, HELLOOO, CRANIUM!
KRACKK
Uggh!
EYE, MEET--
BOFF
STABB
OWWW!
AAAAHH!
YOU PUSBUCKETS GOT NO SOCIAL GRACES!
SHHHKK
*

CRAZY BITCH!
WOAH, THERE, STABBY MCNABB!

WHEN I'M DONE WITH YOU, TART...YOU'RE GONNA LOOK LIKE... SOMEBODY STEPPED IN A BLACKBERRY... AN' STRAWBERRY... PIE!

I DON' THINK SO, YA BIG BAG A' BOOGERS!
RRRKK
KLIKK

CHAPMAN? Uh...HE'S OUT TODAY. I'M HIS FILL-IN.
THAT'S NICE. OPEN THE DOOR. WE GOTTA DO THE ROUNDS.
Uh... OKAY. FIRST, ARE YOU GOOD GUARDS OR BAD GUARDS?

WHATTA YOU MEAN? LIKE GOOD, DO WE DO OUR JOB?
OR BAD, WE SLEEP DURING SHIFTS? OR ABUSE OUR UNION GUIDELINES?
CAN YOU TAKE A SECOND TO CLARIFY WHAT EXACTLY YOU ARE ASKIN'?
WAIT A MINUTE, I REMEMBER YOU...

UH-OH!
HERE, HAVE SOME TASTY MACE FOR YOUR PASTY FACE!
EEEYYAAARRGH!!

CODE RED IN SECTOR 8!
SHUT THE PLACE DOWN AND GET BACK-UP HERE, N--
KAFF KAFF
PAFF
...OOOWW!

I REMEMBER YOU, TOO, EDDIE, AND THIS...
GUUUHH
...IS FOR THAT!

RRRNNT! RRRNNT! RRRNNT! RRRNNT!
ANYBODY ELSE?
...YOU GOTTA GO, RIGHT NOW!
HARLEY...
DAMN.
WE GOT A TON OF COPS HEADING YOUR WAY!
GUYS, IF YOU CAN HEAR ME...

HARLEY, WE GOTTA GET THE HELL OUT OF HERE. YOU HEARD WHAT SHE SAID.
I CAN'T MOVE HIM. HIS INJURIES ARE REALLY BAD.
THEN LET THEM TAKE CARE OF HIM.
WHAT?? NO!
IF I LEAVE 'IM, THEY'LL KILL 'IM. YOU HEARD WHAT THE GUARD SAID UP FRONT.
I DIDN'T COME THIS FAR TA FAIL!
LOOK, THE REGULAR POLICE ARE COMING. THEY CAN'T ALL BE KILLERS ON THE TAKE. ODDS ARE THEY'LL RUSH HIM TO A HOSPITAL. I BOUGHT US SOME TIME AT THE FRONT DESK, BUT...
HARLEY, I CAN'T AFFORD TO DO ANOTHER STRETCH IN THIS PLACE.
PLEASE.
HE...HE'S RIGHT. YOU GOTTA... GOTTA GET OUTTA HERE...THEY'LL ARREST YOU.
PLEASE.

DAMN.
I HATE WHEN EVERYONE ELSE IS RIGHT.

OKAY, I GOT A PLAN. A REALLY GOOD ONE.
HANG IN THERE FER ME. WE GOT SOME ALONE TIME COMIN' TO US.
THIS WAY! SOMEONE OPEN THAT DAMN DOOR!
IT'S WELDED SHUT! IS THERE ANOTHER WAY IN?
NO! SOMEONE GET A BLOWTORCH!
AW, CRAP. THEY'RE ALWAYS BARGIN' IN ON OUR BUSINESS.
MASON...
...I WILL GET YOU OUTTA HERE!
IT'S A DATE.

I'M GONNA TIE SOME TOURNIQUETS TA STOP MASON'S BLEEDIN'.
YOU GRAB ANOTHER ONE A' THESE BOZOS AN' MAKE A BLOOD TRAIL LEADIN' BACK HERE, SO WHOEVER COMES IN FINDS MASON QUICKLY. UNNERSTAND?

GOT IT. THEN WHAT? WE GOT A WALL OF COPS HEADING OUR WAY.

HARLEY QUEENS IS GONNA BLOW OUT THE BACK WALL, AN' WE ALL JUMP IN THE VAN TO GO SEE A MAN ABOUT A PRISONER. ISN'T THAT RIGHT?

LOUD AND CLEAR, BOSS. SAW THIS COMING, AND WAITING FOR YOUR SIGNAL.

DO IT!
INCOMING!

BA-BLOOOEEY
NICE SHOT! TIME TO VACATE THIS JOINT!

OKEE-DOKEE...

...ONE MORE TIME, WARDEN.

AS SOON AS YOU GUYS LEAVE, I WAIT FIFTEEN MINUTES... THEN MAKE A CALL TO MAKE SURE THE PRISONER... MASON MACABRE... IS TRANSFERRED OUT OF MY PRISON...

...AND INTO A PRISON -munch- OUTTA STATE...
...SAFE AND SOUND...
...OR I WILLLLL...

Oh, DO I HAVE TO REPEAT IT?
Mmm-Hmm...
VERY WELL.
OR YOU WILL COME HERE ONE NIGHT, WHEN I AM SOUND ASLEEP...
...KIDNAP MY CHILDREN AND MAKE THEM WORK FOR A SIDESHOW...
...AND TIE MY WIFE AND I TO THE BED AND LIGHT IT ON FIRE.

RIIIGHT, -chomp- BUT NOT BEFORE I...

NOT BEFORE YOU...?!?
WAIT! YOU DIDN'T SAY ANYTHING ELSE! ISN'T THAT ENOUGH??

Hmmm...
GLUG GLUG
...Heh! I GUESS SO.
I MUST BE SLIPPIN'.
WELL, AS LONG AS WE'RE CLEAR ON EVERYTHING, I WON'T TAKE UP ANY MORE A' YER TIME.

OKAY, GANG. THIS FINE FAMILY HAS HAD ENOUGH EXCITEMENT FER ONE NIGHT. TIME TA SAY BYE-BYE!
CAN I JUST FINISH THIS LEVEL? I'M SO CLOSE.
HARV... YOU'RE SUCKING AT THIS!
AW, I'M KICKING BOTH A' YOUR TUSHES.
I WANNA WORK FOR A SIDESHOW...

DO I NEED TA TURN AROUND?
NOPE. HE JUST CALLED THE PRISON AS YOU ASKED. LOST THE SIGNAL AFTER THAT, BUT WE'RE FAR AWAY ENOUGH THAT THEY'LL NEVER FIND US.
OKAY, I'M TEXTING TONY THAT WE'RE HEADING BACK.
SO, WAS IT ME, OR WAS I SEEING THE START OF A BEAUTIFUL RELATIONSHIP BACK IN THE PRISON SHOWER?

I GOTTA SAY, IT BROKE MY HEART LEAVIN' MASON THERE LIKE THAT.
YOU SAID IT YOURSELF. IF WE MOVED HIM HE WOULD BE IN WORSE SHAPE.
SO, WHAT'S WITH YOU AND THE BAD BOYS?
AW, MASON'S KINDA NOT REALLY A BAD BOY. AN' Y'KNOW, Y'CAN'T HELP WHAT YA FEEL AND WHO YA FEEL IT WITH.
HMPH. I WISH OTHER PEOPLE WOULD BE SO OPEN-MINDED. MY LIFE WOULD'VE BEEN A LOT EASIER, THAT'S FOR SURE.

SHOULDN'T WE JUST BE GOING AFTER WHOEVER PUT THE HIT ON MASON?
I ALREADY KNOW IT'S THE MAYOR. HE WANTS REVENGE FOR HIS SON'S DEATH, EVEN IF IT WAS AN ACCIDENT.
HE'S DOIN' WHAT A LOTTA PARENTS WOULD DO IF SOMEONE HURT THEIR KID...HURTIN' 'EM RIGHT BACK.

I REALLY SHOULDN'T BLAME HIM, BUT I STILL WANNA KILL 'IM. I GUESS WE'LL HAVE TA HAVE ANOTHER TALK.
I'M IN A TOUGH SPOT, 'CAUSE HE'S KEEPING THE OTHER PART A' THE BARGAIN, WHICH IS TA LEAVE YOU AN' THE REST A' THE GANG ALONE.
LET'S HOPE WHEREVER THEY MOVED MASON IS SAFER THAN WHERE HE WAS.

HARLEY... ->snff<- ...MY SON!
MADAME MACABRE! WHAT'S GOIN' ON?
Uh-oh.
Muh... MASON... HE'S...
WHAT? WHAT HAPPENED???

THEY SAID HE WAS HURT ->sob<- AND GETTING TREATMENT...
...AND THEN THEY MOVED HIM TO ANOTHER PRISON.
THAT'S GREAT NEWS! HE HADDA GET OUTTA THERE. WHERE DID THEY MOVE HIM TO?

TO GOTHAM.
THEY PUT MY SON IN ARKHAM ASYLUM!
Aw, CRAP.

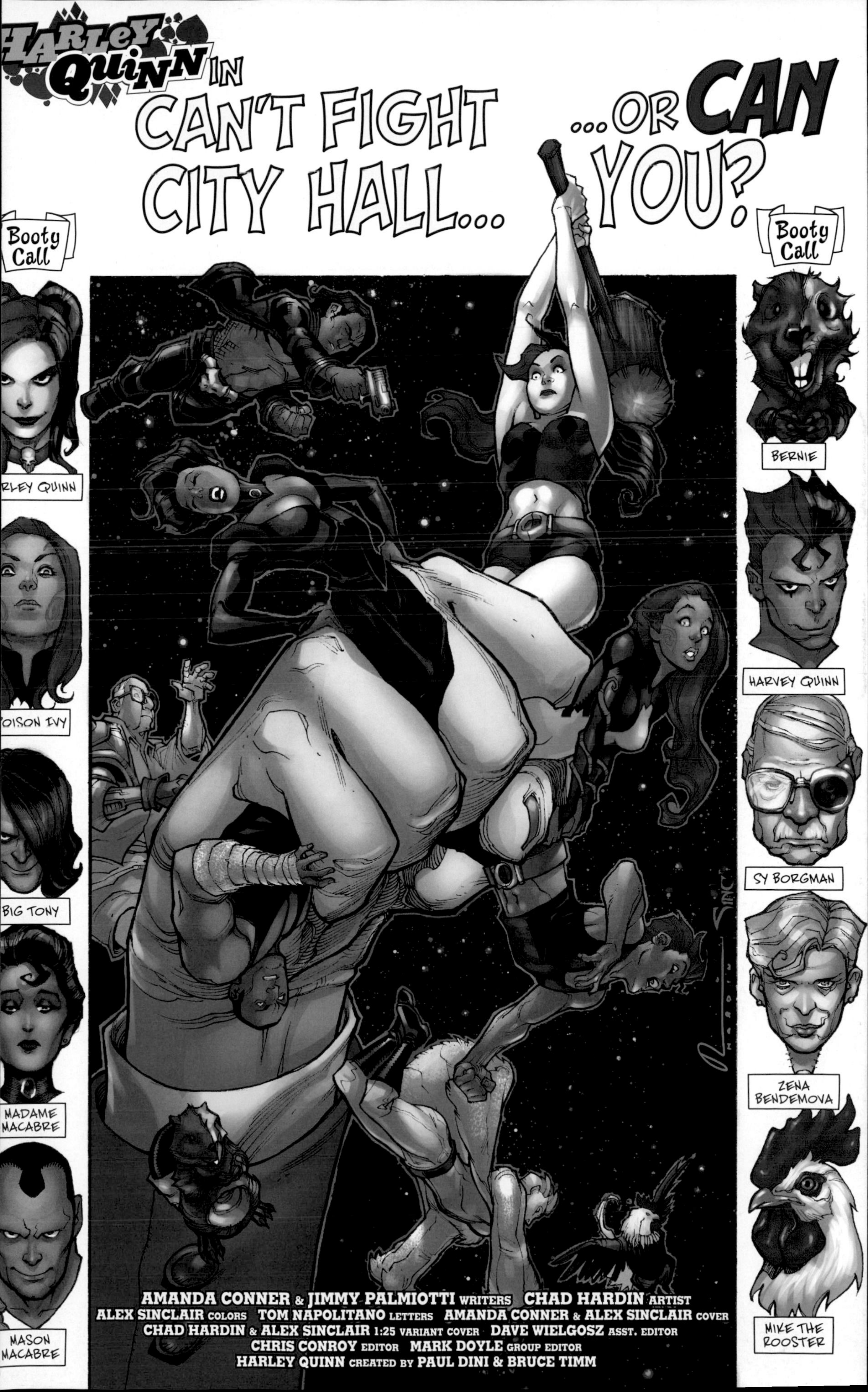
HARLEY QUINN IN
CAN'T FIGHT CITY HALL...
...OR CAN YOU?
Booty Call
RLEY QUINN
OISON IVY
BIG TONY
MADAME MACABRE
MASON MACABRE
Booty Call
BERNIE
HARVEY QUINN
SY BORGMAN
ZENA BENDEMOVA
MIKE THE ROOSTER
AMANDA CONNER & JIMMY PALMIOTTI WRITERS CHAD HARDIN ARTIST
ALEX SINCLAIR COLORS TOM NAPOLITANO LETTERS AMANDA CONNER & ALEX SINCLAIR COVER
CHAD HARDIN & ALEX SINCLAIR 1:25 VARIANT COVER DAVE WIELGOSZ ASST. EDITOR
CHRIS CONROY EDITOR MARK DOYLE GROUP EDITOR
HARLEY QUINN CREATED BY PAUL DINI & BRUCE TIMM

CITY HALL, MANHATTAN.
OOOFFF!!
...FER THE LAST TIME, I'M GONNA SEE YER BOSS.
AND FOR THE LAST TIME--
AAAGHHH--!
--NO WAY IN HELL!
YOU NEED AN APPOINTMENT TO SEE HIS HONOR.
HE AIN'T THE POPE, AN' THE CONGENIALITY BOAT SAILED EVER SINCE YER BOSS TRIED TA HAVE MY BUDDY MASON WHACKED IN JAIL.
Queens
YOU HAVE NO PROOF OF THIS!
WHAT THE HELL IS GOING ON IN HERE?!?
SHE DIDN'T HAVE AN APPOINTMENT...
AN' I WAS PULPABLY LETTIN' HIM KNOW THAT I DID.
YOU AN' ME, MISTAH MAYOR... WE GOTTA TALK.
CECIL, CANCEL MY APPOINTMENTS AND GET FIVE OF OUR BEST OFFICERS OVER HERE NOW.
JUST IN CASE THIS LUNATIC GIVES ME ANY TROUBLE.
Y'BETTER MAKE IT TWENNY.
YOU HEARD HER. MAKE THIS HAPPEN RIGHT NOW.

MS. QUINN, I WOULD LIKE YOU TO *LOOK* AT THIS PHOTO. WHAT DO YOU *SEE?*
PLEASE. WHAT DO YOU SEE?
WE PLAYIN' *WHERE'S WALDO?*

WHITE RIVILEGE?
AND...
YOU WITH A VERY HANDSOME MALE LOVER?
DON'T BE *CRASS.* THAT WAS MY SON, *MICHAEL.*
YOUR *"FRIEND"* KILLED HIM IN A BAR FIGHT.

ACCIDENT OR NOT, HE REMAINS *DEAD,* AND YOUR "FRIEND" WILL *STAY* IN JAIL AND SERVE HIS *TIME.*
THERE IS NOTHING YOU CAN DO ABOUT THAT. IT'S THE *LAW.*
EVEN IF YOU *DO* TRY TO HELP HIM ESCAPE, HE WILL BE ON THE RUN UNTIL HE IS *CAUGHT,* WHICH INEVITABLY WILL HAPPEN.

SURE. WHY BOTHER. PAY A FEW MEN TA *OFF* 'IM WHILE HE'S IN JAIL AND *THAT'S* THAT, RIGHT? WELL, IT *DIDN'T WORK.* MASON'S *ALIVE,* AN' BEING TRANSFERRED TO *ARKHAM ASYLUM* IN *GOTHAM.*
THAT'S WHY I'M *HERE*...TA CUT A *DEAL* WITH YOU.
YA MESSED HIM UP *ENOUGH* AN' MADE YER *POINT.* WHY DON'T WE CALL IT *QUITS* AN' FIGURE OUT A WAY TO PUT ALL THIS TA *REST?*

WE BOTH KNOW *NOTHIN'LL* BRING YER SON BACK. WRECKIN' SOMEBODY ELSE'S LIFE PROBABLY ISN'T THE LEGACY YOU WANNA LEAVE BEHIND IN HIS NAME, AN' *I KNOW* YOU KNOW THE DIFFERENCE BETWEEN AN *ACCIDENT* AN' *MANSLAUGHTER.*
LOOK, MASON FEELS *HORRIBLE* ABOUT WHAT HAPPENED. GET HIM OUTTA THE SYSTEM. FIGURE OUT SOMETHIN' ELSE HE CAN DO TA MAKE IT UP TA YOU.
I *GUARANTEE* IT'LL BE BETTER FOR *ALL PARTIES INVOLVED.*

HAVE YOU EVER HAD A CHILD, MS. QUINN? I DON'T THINK SO. BECAUSE OF THIS, I KNOW YOU WILL NEVER FULLY UNDERSTAND THE GRIEF I FEEL.
I LOST A HUGE CHUNK OF MYSELF WHEN MICHAEL LEFT US. MY WIFE IS DEPRESSED. SHE'S TAKEN TO DRINKING HER PAIN AWAY, AND NEVER TALKS TO ME, OR LEAVES THE HOUSE.
YET, I HAVE TO COME IN HERE DAY AFTER DAY, AND SMILE FOR THE CAMERAS AND TELL EVERYONE THEIR CHAOTIC CITY IS DOING FINE AND IS ALL UNDER CONTROL.
AS FAR AS MASON MACABRE, I HAVE NOTHING TO DO WITH ANYTHING HAPPENING IN JAIL, AND EVEN LESS WITH GETTING HIM TRANSFERRED FROM NEW YORK TO GOTHAM. THIS IS ALL NEWS TO ME.
IF IT'S TRUE, I UNDERSTAND HOW YOU'D THINK IT'S ME, BUT I SWEAR ON MY SON'S SOUL, I AM NOT THE CAUSE OF HIS PRISON PROBLEMS.
I WILL TELL YOU IT WAS ME THAT INTERRUPTED YOUR ROMANTIC DINNER AND PUT HIM BACK IN LOCK-UP WHERE HE BELONGS. HE WAS A FUGITIVE AND YOU KNEW IT.
NOW, ALL THAT SAID, I HARDLY FEEL BAD FOR HIM. HONESTLY, I PROBABLY WOULD BE ABLE TO GET HIM OUT OF ARKHAM AND TRANSFERRED BACK UPSTATE, BUT I'M NOT LIFTING A FINGER. I DON'T OWE YOU OR HIM A THING.
I HAVE TAPES A' YOU TAKIN' BRIBES. REMEMBER?
YES, AND WE HAVE A DEAL.
SO, TAKE THIS CIGAR AND STICK IT, AND WHILE YOU'RE AT IT, STICK TO THE DEAL WE MADE ABOUT YOUR GANG OF HARLEYS...
...THEN DO ME A FAVOR AND GET LOST.
THOOMP
AND THE NEXT TIME YOU FEEL YOU HAVE TO SEE ME, JUST CALL.
MY SCHEDULE IS BOOKED FOR THE NEXT FEW YEARS.

LOOK, I FEEL BAD ABOUT YER SON. I REALLY DO.
THE DEATH OF A KID IS DEVASTATIN'. I GET THAT.
BUT... I'M GONNA GET MASON OUTTA ARKHAM WITH OR WITHOUT YER HELP. HE'S A GOOD GUY. HE UNDERSTANDS WHAT HE DID AND SERIOUSLY REGRETS IT.
THERE'S NO REASON TA HAVE MORE BLOOD ON YER HANDS, BUT IF THAT'S THE WAY IT'S GONNA BE...
SKRNCH

I WON'T HAVE A DROP OF BLOOD ON MY HANDS. I ALREADY TOLD YOU IT WASN'T ME DOING THIS. THAT'S THE TRUTH, WHETHER YOU LIKE IT OR NOT.
DO WHAT YOU MUST. I'M NOT THE ONE TO WORRY ABOUT.

MAKE ONE MOVE, QUINN...JUST ONE AND YOU GET IT.

OH YEAH?
PPHHHTTHHH!
DO YERSELF A FAVOR AN' HOOK UP WITH A MAD SCIENTIST, SO'S SHE CAN GROW YOU A SPINE, CECIL.

GLAD YA MADE IT OUT ALIVE. FIGURED I'D RUN IN WHEN I HEARD GUNSHOTS.
SO? WHAT DID HE SAY?
HE SAID HE DIDN'T ORDER A HIT ON HIM...AN' I BELIEVE HIM. I DO HAVE MY SUSPICIONS, THOUGH.

BACK TA SQUARE ONE.
LET'S GO HOME, TONY. I GOT SOME CALLS TA MAKE.

YOU WANTED TO SEE ME, SIR?
YOU HAVE SOMETHING YOU WANT TO TELL ME, CECIL?
HOW DO YOU MEAN?
YOU'VE BEEN MAKING MOVES BEHIND MY BACK, HAVEN'T YOU?
YOU KNOW ONLY MY OFFICE CAN OKAY A TRANSFER OF AN INMATE TO ANOTHER FACILITY.
COME CLEAN OR CONSIDER YOURSELF FIRED.
SIR, I THOUGHT IT WOULD BRING YOU SOME CLOSURE...AND IF I TOLD YOU, YOU WOULD'VE BEEN LIABLE.
WELL, NOW YOU'VE TOLD ME AND NOW I AM. I'VE GOT A BIGGER PROBLEM THAN MACABRE, WITH THAT HARLEY CHARACTER AND THE BLACKMAIL MATERIAL SHE HAS ON OUR OFFICE.
CONSIDER IT TAKEN CARE OF, SIR. WHAT I WILL DO IS...
STOP. JUST DO IT. I DON'T NEED TO KNOW.

CONEY ISLAND.
SO WHAT'S THE PLAN, BOSS?
WELL, WE SURE AREN'T GETTIN' ANY MUNICIPAL HELP.

LOOKS LIKE I'M GONNA HAVE TA DROP BY ARKHAM AN' LIBERATE 'IM ALL BY MY LITTLE BITTY SELF.
LISTEN, PEACHES, WE'RE HERE TA HELP.
HE'S RIGHT. I CAN'T JUST SIT HERE PLAYING WITH YOUR ROOSTER ALL DAY. LET'S GO BUST HIM OUT!
I'M READY TO DO WHATEVER IT TAKES.
ARE YOU ALL MESHUGENAH?? SHE SAID ARKHAM ASYLUM! THAT PLACE IS PRACTICALLY IMPENETRABLE.

SY'S RIGHT. I'VE BEEN THERE AND KNOW THE PLACE BETTER'N ANYONE.

SOME A' YOU MIGHT NOT KNOW IT, BUT I GOT HISTORY WITH THAT PLACE...
...AN' SOME A' THE INMATES, TOO.
YEAH, WHO DOESN'T?

I WAS A DOCTOR THERE YEARS AGO AN' I KNOW ALL ABOUT THEIR PROTOCOL.
I THINK THIS IS SOMETHIN' I'M GONNA HAVE TO DO ALONE.
THANK GOD!

I JUST COULDN'T PUT ANY A' YOU IN THAT KIND A' DANGER. THE PLACE IS FILLED WITH SOME A' THE MOST DANGEROUS CRIMINALS AN' MURDERERS ON THE PLANET.
SERIOUSLY? TAKE A LOOK AROUND THIS ROOM.
SERIOUSLY. IN ORDER TA DO THIS, I GOTTA GET SOME LOCAL TALENT TA GIMME A HAND.

WHAT I NEED YA ALL TA DO IS TRUST ME AN' COVER MY ASS WHILE I'M AWAY.
NO VORRIES, DARLEENK.

MY PLAN IS TA GO IN, CHURN UP SOME CHAOS, AN' GET HIM OUT IN ONE PIECE.
I GOTTA LEAVE TONIGHT. I'LL HAVE A TRACKIN' DEVICE ON ME, SO IF YA DON'T HEAR FROM ME, YOU CAN FIND ME...
...BUT NO ONE COMES LOOKIN' FER ME 'TIL I'M AWOL FER FORTY-EIGHT HOURS, THAT CLEAR?

CLEAR AS A BELL.
Uh... I'M SORRY TO INTERRUPT, BUT IT LOOKS LIKE WE HAVE TROUBLE HEADING OUR WAY.

Aw, jeez. WHO DID WE PISS OFF THIS WEEK?
WE'LL FIGURE THAT OUT LATER. ALL OUR BUDDIES DOWNSTAIRS ARE GONNA NEED OUR PROTECTION.
EVERYONE BUT SY AN' BERNIE, GET INSIDE MY CLOSET.
SY, BERNIE, GUARD THE DOOR.
WHAT?? HEY, FRUITCAKES! WHAT, AM I S'POSED TA GNAW THEIR LEGS OFF 'TIL THEY FALL OVER?
WAIT, DID YOU SAY "INSIDE"?
LISSEN TO HER.
I DIDN'T THINK HIDING WAS YOUR THING.
AAAWKK!
IT ISN'T.
HANG ON.
BEEP

EEYAAAHH!!!
WOOOOOO!!

...
Uhh...
BOK
MMMPHH
HOLEE JUMBLED ANATOMOLEE!!!

HOT-DIGGETY HEAVY ARTILLERY! HOW D'YA LIKE THE BASEMENT ARSENAL?
EVERYONE PULL OUTTA THE DUNGEON PLUNGE OKAY?
IT WENT BETTER THAN I EXPECTED.
REALLY? I FEEL LIKE MY ASS WAS SAND-PAPERED!
MY ZHOPA MADE SPARKS ON ZE VAY DOWN!

OKAY, EVERYBODY GRAB A WEAPON.
TONY, GET THE CAMERAS UP AN' RUNNING.
ALREADY DONE, DOLL.

WE GOT A DOZEN HITTIN' THE BUILDING FROM ALL DIRECTIONS. THEY LOOK LIKE THEY MEAN BUSINESS.
THIS IS A SHOOT-TA-KILL SITUATION, FOLKS.

TRY TA KEEP SOME OF 'EM ALIVE. I WANNA QUESTION 'EM, AN' FIND OUT WHO SENT 'EM. EVERYBODY READY?
SO, WE SHOOT THEM IN THE FAMILY JEWELS?
OR ZE KNEES...
HARLEY, WE GOTTA GO! MY FREAKSHOW CREW IS GETTIN' READY FOR TONIGHT'S SHOW, AN' THEY HAVE NO CLUE WHAT'S COMING.

SNEAK ATTACK!

ZIS ATTACK? IT IS NOT SO SNEAKY.
YEAH, I THINK THEY HEARD 'ER SCREAM ALL THE WAY IN JERSEY.

YOU THREE GO TO THE SECOND FLOOR AND WE'LL TAKE THE THIRD. THE REST OF THE BOYS ARE SWEEPING THE APARTMENTS.
KILL ANYTHING WITH A PULSE. WHEN YER DONE, CALL IN THE TORCH TO FINISH THE JOB.
HEY! BUT NUGGET

KNNCHH
SKSSHH
GHAAAA!!
WHOOPSIE DAISIES! I THINK THAT MIGHTA ENDED YOU.
JINKIES, I DUNNO MY OWN STRENGTH!

SO MANY PLACES FOR SHOOTING.
TRY TO STAND STILL NOW...MY ARM GEARS, ZEY ARE A BIT SHAKY.

BLAM
BLAM

DISARM AND DAT ARM. GET IT?

HOW'S THAT HEM COMING ALONG?
ALMOST DONE, QUEENIE. I'M TRIPLE STITCHIN' IT SO WE WON'T HAVE TO DO THIS AGAIN.
HEY, I WANNA THANK YOU FOR LETTING ME TRY OUT TONIGHT.
WE'RE HAPPY TO HAVE YOU, KIDDO. IT'S GOOD TO KEEP A STEADY ROTATION OF NEW TALENT TO KEEP THE REGULARS HAPPY AS WELL.
THWAPP
YIII

WHADDA WE HAVE HERE? ALL MY FANTASIES COME TRUE!
DUDE...WE HAVE TO KILL THEM, REMEMBER?

WHO SAYS WE CAN'T HAVE SOME FUN FIRST.

I DO!

KNNCHH
?!
BAH!

TAKE THAT, YA FREAK!
KRAKK

Ghaahhh... BY DOZE!
ENOUGH OF THIS. SAY 'BYE, TOUGH GUY!
WAIT!
FOR WHAT?

FOR THESE!
BERRY CHRISTBAS!
RRRRRFF!
ROW!
BA-BOOM

Oh my God, THE SIGHT OF OUR BODACIOUS BOOBIES MADE THEIR HEADS EXPLODE!
OKAY, THAT'S NEVER HAPPENED BEFORE.
NO NEED TA BE SHY, LADIES...I'VE SEEN IT ALL.

TONY!
DO ME A SOLID, WILL YA? SECURE THE DOOR BEHIND ME. WE'RE ON LOCKDOWN.
WE'LL BE BACK LATER TO COLLECT THE CARCASSES.

ZIS IS GETTING US NOWHERE. COVER ME.
WAIT! WHAT ARE YOU GONNA DO?
ROLLERBALL!
POM POM POM
PAF
PAF
PAF
PAF
PAF

POEKHALI!

PCHING
PAF
PAF

A-BOOM
BADA-BOOOM

T WAS THE MOST PECTACULAR HING I HAVE EVER SEEN.
I VAS GYMNAST VEN I VAS YOUNG GIRL IN KRASNODAR. YOU SHOULD HAF SEEN ME IN ACTION.
I JUST DID AND IT WAS AMAZING!
COULD YOU TEACH ME TO DO THAT?

BLIZOK LOKOTOK, DA NE UKUSISH--YOUR ELBOW IS CLOSE, YES? YET YOU CANNOT BITE IT.
I AM COMPLETELY LOST. ELBOW BITING?
TRANSLATION, IT ONLY SEEMS EASY. IT IS NOT.
VIZ MUCH PRACTICE, AND ARMOR PLATING, I ZINK YOU CAN, EVENTUALLY.
YOU LOOK QUITE BENDY FOR A BOY.

I JUST WANT TO DO EVERYTHING IN MY LIFETIME, Y'KNOW WHAT I MEAN, ZENA?
FOR BIG SHIP, BIG VOYAGE. WE GO DOWN TO SEE HOW ZE OTHERS DID NOW, YES?
SURE, MAMA.

THIS PLACE CREEPS ME OUT. ALL WAX MUSEUMS DO. THEY'RE JUST CREEPY IN GENERAL.
I THINK IT'S AN ART FORM, HOW SOMEONE CAN USE WAX TO MAKE SOMETHIN' THAT LOOKS SO REALISTIC.
THIS IS A WAX MUSEUM OF SERIAL KILLERS. WHO WANTS TO SEE THAT?
WELL, LET'S BE HONEST. ALL OF US KINDA BELONG HERE IN A WAY, RIGHT?
WE KILL FOR MONEY. THESE GUYS KILL FOR FUN.
I KILL FOR FUN. WH
YOU GUYS DO
LIKE THIS JO
Oh, I DO. I MEAN, IMAGINE BEING LOOKED UP TO ONE DAY, LIKE THESE GUYS ARE... IT'S KINDA COOL.
NO, IT IS NOT. THIS IS NOT HERE TO GLORIFY THEM. IT IS A WARNING.
IDIOTS.
DEAD IDIOTS.
BLAM BLAM BLAM

HE SAID TO KILL EVERYTHING WITH A PULSE. TAKE OUT THE ANIMALS.
WHAT? ARE YOU KIDDING? I'M NOT SHOOTING INNOCENT PUPPIES AND KITTENS.
...WHO WILL GROW UP TO BE VICIOUS ANIMALS WITH BLOOD-LUST.
YARF
PRRR?
I'M WITH HARRY. I DON'T KILL ANIMALS UNLESS I'M GONNA EAT 'EM OR THEY ATTACK ME.
SEEMS ALL THESE LITTLE FELLAS WANT IS TO BE PETTED.
WAIT A SECOND. YOU GUYS SEE WHAT I'M SEEING?

PANT PANT
IT'S FRIGGIN' DOGZILLA!
LOOK AT HIS MOUTH!

WHAT THE--?

CHOOM
CHOOM
CHOOM
CHOOM

YOU CAN GET OUTTA THE SUIT NOW, TONY.
Uhh... NO I CAN'T.
WHAT?
I HAD A HARD TIME FITTING IN HERE. THE SUIT WAS A LITTLE TIGHT, SO I HAD TO LOSE THE CLOTHING.

Aww, IS BIG TONY A LITTLE SHY?
HARDLY. ALTHOUGH NOW THIS SUIT IS MAKIN' IT FEEL INSECURE.
FINE... LET'S TIE THESE BOZOS UP AN' SEE HOW EVERYBODY'S DOIN'.
*

Feh! I CAN HEAR YOU OUT THERE. DON'T MAKE ME USE THIS MISSILE LAUNCHER THING!
SY, IT'S ME! HARLEY!
ANYONE CAN SAY THAT. HOW DO I KNOW IT'S YOU? TELL ME SOMETHING ONLY HARLEY QUINN WOULD KNOW ABOUT ME!

YOU USED TO BE A SUPERSPY. YOU HAVE AN ENEMY NAMED IGOR LENIVETSKIN. YER COOT SCOOTER LAUNCHES BAGEL GRENADES. A SEAGULL DROPPED A RUSSIAN SPY'S SEVERED HEAD INTO YER LAP WHILE WE WERE IN CONEY ISLAND.
IT WAS AN EAGLE!
-sigh- FINE. Y'WANT ME TA GO ON?

WHAT'S MY FAVORITE COLOR?

13
!?!

Ummm... RHODAMINE?
THAT'S IT!
COME IN, PLEASE.

WELL, BY
HEAD COUNT, AN' A MISSING HEAD-OUNT, WE GOT EIGHT DEAD KILLERS AND TWELVE LIVE ONES. NOT TOO SHABBY.
FER YOU GUYS THAT ARE ALIVE, THE FIRST ONE THAT TELLS ME WHO HIRED YA GETS TO STAY ALIVE. THE REST A' YOU WILL BE KICKIN' THE BUCKET IN A HORRIBLE FASHION THAT WE HAVEN'T BEEN CREATIVE ENOUGH TA FIGURE OUT YET.
SO. WHO'S GONNA RAT OUT THEIR BOSS?

CECIL FROM THE MAYOR'S OFFICE!
I'LL NEVER TELL!
Uhh... DIDJA SEE WHICH ONE WAS FIRST?
I DUNNO. THEY ALL YELLED IT AT THE SAME TIME, EXCEPT FOR THAT ONE GUY NOT TELLIN'.
Uh-oh. SO HOW DOES THIS WORK?
IT'S YOUR CALL.

SO, YA SAID YOU'LL NEVER TELL, BUT LIKE ME, YA WITNESSED YER FELLOW HIT MEN RATTIN' OUT THE GUY THAT HIRED YOU.
HOW'S THAT MAKE YA FEEL?
I'M ASHAMED OF WHAT HAS BECOME OF THIS PROFESSION.

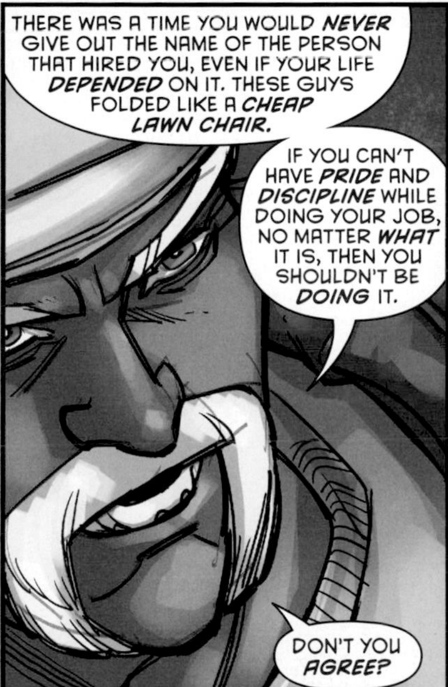
THERE WAS A TIME YOU WOULD NEVER GIVE OUT THE NAME OF THE PERSON THAT HIRED YOU, EVEN IF YOUR LIFE DEPENDED ON IT. THESE GUYS FOLDED LIKE A CHEAP LAWN CHAIR.
IF YOU CAN'T HAVE PRIDE AND DISCIPLINE WHILE DOING YOUR JOB, NO MATTER WHAT IT IS, THEN YOU SHOULDN'T BE DOING IT.
DON'T YOU AGREE?

YEAH! THE WAY THE REST A' THESE GUYS JUST GAVE UP SO EASILY IS EMBARRASSIN' ON A NUMBER A' LEVELS. YOU MUST FEEL VERY DISAPPOINTED AND ISOLATED RIGHT NOW.
Hmmm...
ALL RIGHT, I MADE A DECISION, FOLKS...

THUMMP
Huh?
?!
WHAT IN BLAZES--?
THUMP
THUMP
THUMP
GET DOWN!
KRRRSHHHH
I THINK IT STOPPED.
WHAT THE HELL IS THIS?
I CAN EXPLAIN.
IS THAT A NOTE STAPLED TO HIS FACE?

HOW 'BOUT *THAT* ONE?
RIGHT THROUGH THE *MAYOR'S WINDOW.* JUST *BEAUTIFUL!*
VE HAFF ONE MORE LEFT...
SEE HOW *EASY* IT IS? Y'WANNA SEND THE LAST GUY?
REALLY? *CAN I??*
ONLY IF YA SWEAR TA *NEVER BOTHER* ME AN' MY FRIENDS *EVER AGAIN.*
YOU HAVE MY *WORD.*

I'M TOO *YOUNG* TO DIE!
HOW OLD ARE YOU?
I TURN FORTY-THREE IN *TWO DAYS.*
Hmm... ZAT'S NOT BAD AGE.

WOO-HOOO!
FLAP YER *ARMS!* YA *MIGHT* HAVE A *CHANCE!*

HIS ARMS VERE *TIED UP,* LAPUSHKA.
Ohh... riiight. THAT'S A *BUMMER.*

LET ME SEE WHAT THIS SAYS...
"THIS MEANS WAR. XOXO, HARLEY."
CECIL...
sigh
I'LL TYPE UP MY RESIGNATION AND HAVE IT FOR YOU IN THE MORNING.
!
AHHHHHHH!!!
KA-THUNNKK
OH GOD! I-I CAN'T BELIEVE IT! I'M STILL ALIVE!
WHAT ARE THE CHANCES??
I'M GONNA GO OUT AND PLAY THE LOTTERY!!!

PENN STATION
MY GUY MADE UP WHAT YA WANTED. I LOOKED 'EM OVER AN' THEY'RE PRETTY DAMN GOOD.

AW, THANKS, TONY.
YOU'D HAVE TA LOOK AT 'EM WITH A MAGNIFYIN' GLASS TA SEE THEY'RE FAKES.
I TRUST YOU.
DIDJA MAKE THE CALLS FOR ME?

MOST OF 'EM. STILL GOT A FEW.
LOOK, HONESTLY, IF YA FIND YERSELF OVER YER HEAD, JUST GIMME A CALL. I GOT FRIENDS EVERYWHERE.

I KNOW. GIMME A HUG AN' STOP WORRYIN'.
Y'KNOW I LOVE YA, KID. I'LL NEVER NOT WORRY.
AWW, MUSIC TA MY EARS.

GOTHAM LINE

ARKHAM ASYLUM
-AHEM.-
SO, WHAT DID YOU DO TO GET YOURSELF INTO OUR FINE ESTABLISHMENT?
WELL...I WAS IN A BAR FIGHT.
I ACCIDENTALLY KILLED A MAN.
THERE ARE NO ACCIDENTS MY FRIEND.
Oh, yeah? WELL DISAGRE
WHICH IS FINE. BUT MURDER ALONE DOESN'T GET ONE A TICKET TO THIS FREAK SHOW.
IT WAS THE MAYOR'S SON IN NEW YORK. THE MAYOR'S SPARING NO EXPENSE TO MAKE ME EXTINCT.
I GUESS MAYBE I GOT TRANSFERRED HERE AS PUNISHMENT?
I DUNNO.
WELL, THAT IS REGRETTABLE.
HAVE YOU ANY FAMILY OR FRIENDS?
I HAVE MY MOTHER... AN OLD FRIEND, TONY... AND A GIRL I JUST STARTED TO SEE.
THOSE IN OUR POSITION CAN BE A BURDEN TO FAMILY. EVEN HARDER IS KEEPING A RELATIONSHIP. IT'S BEEN NEXT TO IMPOSSIBLE FOR ME.
WELL, THIS GIRL IS SPECIAL... DIFFERENT FROM ANYONE I'VE EVER KNOWN. SHE'S SWEET AND DANGEROUS, IF THAT MAKES SENSE.
JUST MY TYPE. TOO BAD YOU BOTH DIDN'T HAVE MORE TIME TOGETHER.
I WOULDN'T BE ALIVE IF IT WEREN'T FOR HARLEY. SHE'S AN AMAZING LADY, BUDDY.
HARLEY...?
KAFF KAFF HACH
WOULD THIS YOUNG LADY'S LAST NAME BE QUINZEL?
ACTUALLY, YEAH. D'YOU KNOW HER?
BETTER THAN ANYONE, MY FRIEND.
BETTER THAN ANYONE.

GOTH
BIG TONY
POISON IVY
MADAME MACABRE
WELCOME BACK TO GOTHAM, BANANA BREAD!
AIEEEEEE!!!
IVY!
I CAN'T BELIEVE YA CAME OUT TA MEET ME!
ARE YOU KIDDING? OF COURSE!
THE JOKER
BATMAN
EDGAR "EGGY" FULLERTON YEUNG
QUEENIE
HARLEY NECESSITIES
WENNY-FIVE BIG ONE$.
AMANDA CONNER & JIMMY PALMIOTTI WRITERS
CHAD HARDIN ARTIST
ALEX SINCLAIR COLORS
TOM NAPOLITANO LETTERS
AMANDA CONNER & ALEX SINCLAIR COVER
DAVE WIELGOSZ ASST. EDITOR
CHRIS CONROY EDITOR
MARK DOYLE GROUP EDITOR
CHAD HARDIN & ALEX SINCLAIR 1:25 VARIANT COVER
NEAL ADAMS, RYAN SOOK, JEROMY COX NEAL ADAMS VARIANT COVER
HARLEY QUINN CREATED BY PAUL DINI & BRUCE TIMM
BATMAN CREATED BY BOB KANE WITH BILL FINGER

TONY CALLED AHEAD AND ASKED ME TO ACQUIRE A FEW THINGS FOR YOU.
HE EXPLAINED YOUR WHOLE INSANE PLAN OF LIBERATING MASON FROM ARKHAM ASYLUM.
FOR THE RECORD, I THINK YOU'RE CRAZY AND SWEET, BUT THIS TIME A LOT MORE CRAZY. YOU KNOW THAT PLACE BETTER THAN ANYONE.
YEAH, YEAH, DANGEROUS ARKHAM... CRAZY SCARY WHATEVER...
HEY, I LOVE WHAT YER WEARIN'. WHERE DIDJA FIND THAT ADORABLE DRESS?
CELINE'S CELLAR, LET'S EAT, AND DON'T CHANGE THE SUBJECT.
I FOUND OUT YOUR BOY MASON WAS IN THE TREATMENT CENTER, BUT GOT FAST-TRACKED TO A CELL IN THE MAIN BUILDING. HE HAS HIMSELF SURROUNDED BY REAL HEAVYWEIGHTS.
IF YOU'RE GOING TO GET TO HIM, YOU HAVE TO GET IN AND OUT QUICKLY.
THIS SPAGHETTI IS AMAZIN'! WHERE'S MY SIDE A' MEATBALLS?
SWEETIE, I THINK YOU'RE GONNA NEED MY HELP ON THIS ONE. YOU CAN'T JUST WALK IN THERE AS YOUR OLD SELF...
DIDJA GET WHAT TONY ASKED FER?
YES, OF COURSE. I EVEN GOT THE BOAT. YOU'LL LOVE IT. IT'S ON LOAN.
THEN YER PART OF THIS IS DONE. SERIOUSLY. I GOT IT SIRRP COVERED. WITH YOUR TOYS AN' MY NEW IDENTITY, THIS OUGHTA BE PRETTY EASY.
JUST GOTTA CHANGE AT YER PLACE, THEN I'M SET.
CAN I ASK YOU A PERSONAL QUESTION?
IT'S ABOUT YOU-KNOW-WHO.
YOU CAN ASK ME ANYTHING, YOU KNOW THAT.
I KNOW I'M STEPPIN' INTA PERILOUS PILES A' POOP HERE, BUT MASON'S IN TROUBLE.
IF I DON'T GET HIM OUTTA THERE, HE'LL BE DEAD IN THE NEXT 24 HOURS.
THE OTHER GUY FROM MY PAST...WELL...I HAVE A SOFT SPOT IN MY HEART FER HIM, AN' AT THE SAME TIME I WANNA KILL HIM.
LET'S JUST SAY IT'S IN EVERYONE'S BEST INTEREST T COMPLETELY AVOI HIM, WHICH IS MY PLAN.
GOOD. I WAS HOPING FOR THAT EXAC ANSWER.
ONE OF MY FAVORITE QUALITIES YOU HAVE IS THE TOT DEVOTION TO T PEOPLE YOU LOVE--
--AND THE UTTER LOATHING YOU HAVE FOR PEOPLE THAT HAVE DONE YOU WRONG.
I FIND IT... CHARMING... EVEN SEXY.
SO WHAT'S BOTHERIN' YOU?

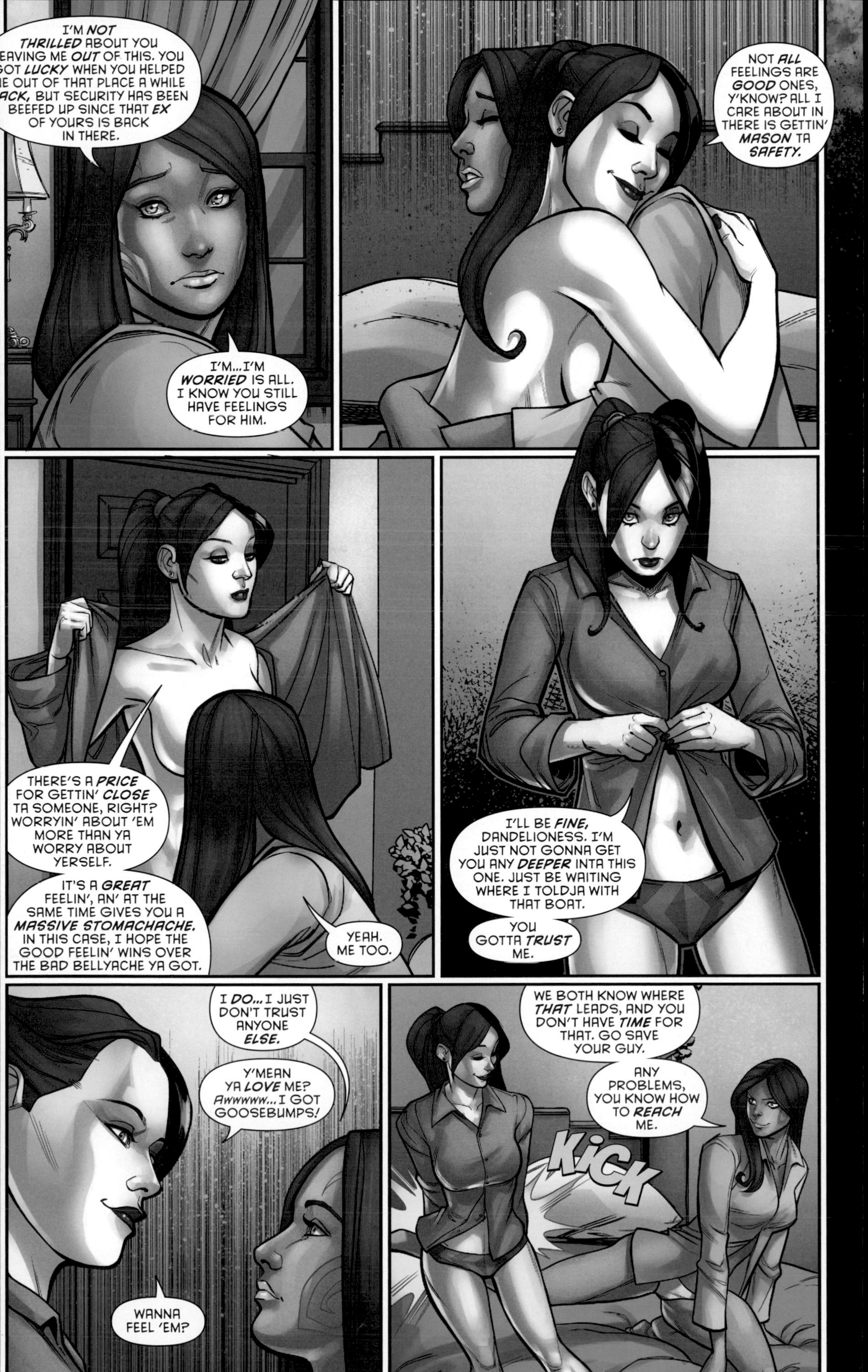
I'M NOT THRILLED ABOUT YOU LEAVING ME OUT OF THIS. YOU GOT LUCKY WHEN YOU HELPED ME OUT OF THAT PLACE A WHILE BACK, BUT SECURITY HAS BEEN BEEFED UP SINCE THAT EX OF YOURS IS BACK IN THERE.
I'M...I'M WORRIED IS ALL. I KNOW YOU STILL HAVE FEELINGS FOR HIM.
NOT ALL FEELINGS ARE GOOD ONES, Y'KNOW? ALL I CARE ABOUT IN THERE IS GETTIN' MASON TA SAFETY.
THERE'S A PRICE FOR GETTIN' CLOSE TA SOMEONE, RIGHT? WORRYIN' ABOUT 'EM MORE THAN YA WORRY ABOUT YERSELF.
IT'S A GREAT FEELIN', AN' AT THE SAME TIME GIVES YOU A MASSIVE STOMACHACHE. IN THIS CASE, I HOPE THE GOOD FEELIN' WINS OVER THE BAD BELLYACHE YA GOT.
YEAH. ME TOO.
I'LL BE FINE, DANDELIONESS. I'M JUST NOT GONNA GET YOU ANY DEEPER INTA THIS ONE. JUST BE WAITING WHERE I TOLDJA WITH THAT BOAT.
YOU GOTTA TRUST ME.
I DO...I JUST DON'T TRUST ANYONE ELSE.
Y'MEAN YA LOVE ME? AWWWWW...I GOT GOOSEBUMPS!
WANNA FEEL 'EM?
WE BOTH KNOW WHERE THAT LEADS, AND YOU DON'T HAVE TIME FOR THAT. GO SAVE YOUR GUY.
ANY PROBLEMS, YOU KNOW HOW TO REACH ME.
KICK

ARKHAM ASYLUM.
Arkham Asylum Visitor Entrance
WHAT ARE THESE PILLS?
DIPHENHYDRAMINE AND DOXYLAMINE. HARMLESS SLEEPING AIDS. YOU SHOULD BE FAMILIAR WITH THESE. MOST OF THE PATIENTS USE THEM ON A DAILY BASIS.
UH, YEAH, DOCTOR. YOU'R CLEAR. GO SEE D FLYNN IN ROOM 122, PLEASE.
DOCTOR SHIPMAN, IT'S AN HONOR TO HAVE YOU HERE. SOMEONE WITH YOUR EXTENSIVE CREDENTIALS SHOULD FIND ARKHAM QUITE INTRIGUING.
WE HOUSE THE WORST OF THE WORST.
DR. FLYNN, I AM WELL AWARE OF ARKHAM'S HISTORY. I KNOW I CERTAINLY CAN MAKE A DIFFERENCE.
IF SOMEONE WOULD SHOW ME TO MY OFFICE, I CAN SET UP AND START TAKING PATIENTS AS SOON AS POSSIBLE.
"THAT'S HARLEEN QUINZEL FOR SURE. NO DOUBT ABOUT IT."

I WAS A NIGHT GUARD WHEN SHE WORKED HERE.
YOU BELIEVE IT? HE WAS ACTUALLY ON THE LEVEL AND RATTED OUT HIS EX. HE MUST REALLY HATE HER.
NOW WHAT? WE ARREST HER?
NAW, SHE'S PRETTY DANGEROUS.
WE GOT HER SETTING UP IN ROOM 134. WE PLUGGED UP THE VENTS AND THERE'S ONLY ONE WAY IN AND OUT.
LET HER GET COMFORTABLE AND THEN WE HIT HER WITH ENOUGH GAS TO CHOKE AN ELEPHANT OUT.

Well, this oughta be fun. The daily roster has Mason not too far from here...
...in the worst offender level.
Oh whoopee.
This little-bitty pill should protect me from the bigger ones' effects.
I hope.
Otherwise, I get my own room at my old haunt.

Okay... I need the freedom ta be myself ta do this right.
Plus, my red an' black is scarier lookin'.
An' it hides bloodstains the best.
Mason, I hope you're ready fer the great escape!
Aw, HOLEE MUG-BUFFERS... GAS MASKS?!
SERIOUSLY?
WELL, HERE GOES NUTHIN'.

HEY QUINN... WE'RE PREPARED, YOU PSYCHO...OR DIDN'T YOU NOTICE?
FLING
POFF
PREPARED FOR THE FOGGIN', MAYBE...
...BUT NOT FOR THE FLOGGIN'.

SNAPP
WHOMPP
Uhhff!
KICKK
Oooff!
-EEEP-
CRUNCHH
CHKK

!
-UHRRKK-

Uhh...
hhh...uhrrr...

...RRRRRAAAHHGG!!!
*

BAFF
HOLEE HOT MESS! THAT GAS PACKS A WALLOP!

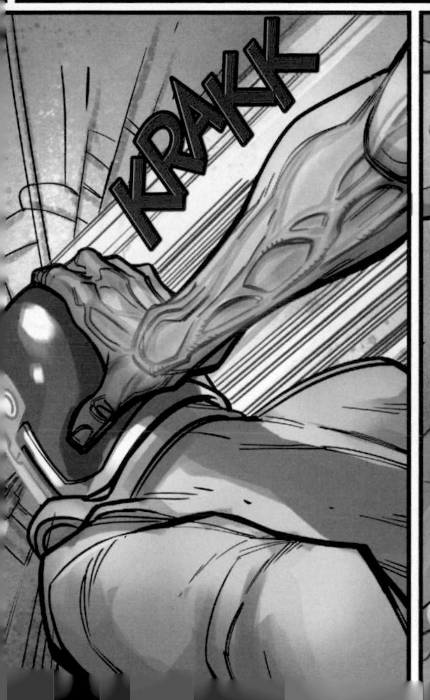
KRAKK

AAHHHRR!
Uuhhh

JEEZ LOWEEZ!
I SHOULDA SKIPPED THAT LI'L PILL AN' JUST FERRIGNOFIED MYSELF!

They know I'm here, which makes this heaps harder.
afeteria
THIS WAY! TAKE HER OUT ANY WAY YOU CAN!

Need a distraction.
toSS
?!

Should get real Animal House in here pretty quickly.

THANK YOU MUCHO.
SNAP

MASON?
MASON!
MAAYYSON!!!

MASON, YOU IN THERE?

HARLEY?!
WHAT ARE YOU DOIN' HERE?
I SAID I'D ETCHA OUT, AN' HERE I AM.
JUST A SEC, I GOT THE KEY...

C'MON, CUTIE! WE GOTTA GET THE HELL OUTTA HERE.
WAIT... HARLEY...
...I HEARD THINGS ABOUT YOU...

...BAD THINGS... FROM ANOTHER INMATE.
AN' YOU BELIEVE 'EM? WHO TOLD YOU?
DOES IT MATTER?

YEAH, IT MATTERS, AN' THE IDEA THAT YOU WOULD BELIEVE 'EM IS JUST...
LOOK, WE DON'T HAVE TIME FOR THIS NOW. WE ONLY HAVE A FEW MINUTES 'TIL THIS PLACE GOES ON COMPLETE LOCKDOWN.

TAKE THIS SMALL PILL AN' HOLD ON TA THESE BIG ONES JUST IN CASE...
...AN' FOLLOW ME.
UH, OKAY.

YOOOO HOOOOO...
HONEY... BABY... PUMPKIN PIE!
AREN'T YOU FORGETTING SOMETHING?

NO NO NO NO NO... NOT HIM.
WALK AWAY. WALK AWAY.
THAT'S THE GUY NEXT DOOR FROM ME...
THE ONE TALKIN' CRAP TO YOU?
YEAH. HORRIBLE THINGS I DON'T WANNA REPEAT.

COME GIVE DADDY A BIG KISS, HARLEY.
YOU KNOW YOU CAN'T RESIST YOUR MAIN MAN.
MASON, LISTEN TA ME...
THERE WAS A TIME IN MY LIFE, WAY BACK WHEN, THAT I'M NOT ESPECIALLY PROUD OF.
I LOST MY WAY AN' PUT MY HEART AN' TRUST INTA SOMEONE SO DARK AND TWISTED...
...WELL, WHEN I WAS WITH HIM, I HAD NOWHERE TA GO BUT UP.
IT'S WHY I LEFT GOTHAM, AN' STARTED A NEW LIFE IN BROOKLYN, WITH A BUNCH OF GOOD, SUPPORTIVE, REAL FRIENDS. PEOPLE WHO HAD MY BACK.

I HAD YOUR BACK, SWEETIE... AMONG OTHER THINGS. WHY DON'T YOU MAKE US BOTH HAPPY AND COME OVER HERE AND LET ME OUT? I PROMISE IT'LL BE WORTH IT.
I KNOW HOW TO MAKE YOU FEEL LIKE YOU AGAIN.

SEE? HE'S REALLY GOOD AT MAKIN' PEOPLE SECOND-GUESS THEMSELVES.
HE'S ONE A' THE MOST MANIPULATIVE PEOPLE ON THIS PLANET.
JUST TRY TA LOOK PAST HIS B.S. AND LOOK AT THE REAL ME.
YOU NEVER MINDED WHEN I MANIPULATED YOU IN THE PAST, SUGAR BOTTOM.
YOU EVEN OWE YOUR SHINY WHITE COMPLEXION TO ME.
C'MON. YOU JUST CAN'T HELP BUT FALL FOR ME OVER AND OVER.
HAHAHAHAHAHAA

NO MATTER WHAT HE SAYS, THAT'S THE OLD ME. THE NEW ME LEARNED WHAT'S IMPORTANT IN THE WORLD AN' IS DOIN' MY BEST TA DO THE RIGHT THING.
YOU CAME HERE TO HELP ME. YOU ALREADY SAVED MY LIFE ONCE.
I'M SORRY IF I EVER BELIEVED A SINGLE WORD HE SAID.
IT'LL NEVER HAPPEN AGAIN.
AWWWW, AND ME WITHOUT A CAMERA.
I THINK I'M GOING TO VOMIT!
OPEN THIS DOOR NOW, YOU RED AND BLACK BIMBO! I MADE YOU WHO YOU ARE TODAY! DON'T FORGET IT.
THAT OVERGROWN GOON ISN'T GOING TO REPLACE THE HOLE IN YOUR HEART THAT I FILL.
THAT'S YOUR OLD BOYFRIEND? HOLY--
HOLEY IS RIGHT... SO MANY HOLES IN YOUR FAT HEAD, YOU COULDN'T FIGURE OUT IT WAS ME 'TIL NOW?
HOLES IN HEARTS... HOLES IN HEADS...
HEY, WATCH YOUR MOUTH OR I'LL RIP IT OFF YOUR FACE.
MASON, I GOT THIS.
8675309
YOU WANT OUTTA YER CAGE?
JUST OPEN THE DOOR AND STOP IT ALREADY. YOU AND I BOTH KNOW WE'RE MEANT TO BE TOGETHER.
TOGETHER?
IT'S AMAZING WHAT A FEW YEARS AN' A LOTTA MILES AWAY FROM YOU AND YER GARBAGE CAN DO FER A GIRL'S SELF-RESPECT.
KLIK

WHAT ARE YOU DOING?
WHAT I SHOULDA DONE A LONG TIME AGO.
UNLOCK THE DOOR.

NO.
WERE GONNA TA
THIS OUT O
AN' FER AL

HARLEY, THAT'S THE JOKER! YOU GOTTA GET OUTTA THERE.
GIMME A COUPLA MINUTES.

I DON'T KNOW WHAT YOUR PLAN IS, QUINZEL--
--BUT BEFORE THIS NIGHT IS OVER, I'M GONNA WRING YOUR SWEET LITTLE NECK 'TIL YOUR EYES POP OUT OF YOUR HEAD!
REMOVE THAT FINGER. NOW.

THAT'S NOT GOING TO HAPPEN. WHAT IS GOING TO HAPPEN IS YOU AND I WILL PLAY A GAME--
--AND YOU'RE GONNA DITCH THAT GORILLA AND LEAVE HERE WITH ME.
DREAM ON. LET'S TALK ABOUT WHAT'S REALLY GOIN' ON HERE.

HAHA. I SEE. IT'S PLAYTIME, JUST LIKE THE OLD DAYS!
WONDERFUL.

OH NO.
NUTHIN LIKE TH OLD DAY "MISTAH

GET YER PASTY PAWS OFF ME!
WHAM
I MAKE THE RULES HERE, PUMPKIN.
AAOOWWW!
STILL FRAIL IN BODY AND IN MIND, HARLEY? SOME THINGS NEVER CHANGE.
I'LL GIVE YOU ONE MORE CHANCE TO MAKE THIS RIGHT.
I GOTCHER "FRAIL" RIGHT HERE!
KRRNCHHH
GHAAAHH!
I GOT THINGS TA BE AN' PLACES TA DO, YA GREEN-HAIRED MONSTER!
DON'T MAKE ME STICK AROUND TA SHOVE MY SHOE UP YOUR BLANCHED BEHIND--
SLAM
WHOPP
Unhff!
YOU JUST CAUSED YOURSELF A WORLD OF PROBLEMS, YOU WITLESS TWIT!

I MAY HAVE A LOTTA PROBLEMS...
BUT YOU...
SCHWOOOP
TRIP

EVERY SINGLE WORD OUTTA YER CACKLIN' YAP, YOU CREATE CHAOS.
HEH. THIS IS NEWS HOW?
I GOT ENOUGH OF IT IN MY OWN HEAD, I DON'T NEED YOU ADDIN' TO IT!

FWAPP
I'M GROWING TIRED OF YOU, QUINN.

YEAH? THE FEELIN' IS MORE THAN MUTUAL.

NO.
NO. IT ISN'T. YOUR FEELINGS COUNT FOR NOTHING, YOU PATHETIC MESS.
WE BOTH KNOW WHAT YOU WANT.

GIVE IN TO IT.

MMMMPH

EEYAAAAGGGHHHH!

PHOO
YER NEVER GONNA MESS WITH ME OR MY MIND AGAIN, YA HEAR ME?
YOU DISGUST ME.

I KNOW.
I DISGUST YOU WHERE IT COUNTS, BABY.

ROT IN HELL, YOU CHUCKLING SCHMUCK.

LET'S SEE WHO GETS THERE FIRST.
NICE KNOWING YOU, QUINN.
-Uuhh... uhh...-

URRRAAAGH!
I HATE YA FER WHAT YA BRING OUT IN ME.
ALL I WANTED TA DO WAS TALK TO YOU...

...AN' HERE WE ARE MUCKIN' AROUND WITH EACH OTHER'S MARBLES...
...AN' POUNDIN' EACH OTHER TO A PULP...
...AS USUAL...
THUNK

...'CAUSE EVERY TIME WE GET TOGETHER, THAT'S WHAT WE DO.
IT'S NOT MY THING...
...I DON' LIKE IT...
KKRRNCHH
...AN' I'M DONE WITH IT.

HARLEY! WE GOT COMPANY ON THE WAY!

USE THE PELLETS, SWEETIE, I'M ALMOST DONE HERE.

I'M NOT YER TOY ANYMORE. UNNERSTAND?
YOU DID MEAN SOMETHIN' TA ME ONE TIME, BUT THAT TIME IS OVER.
IF I EVER HEAR YOU OR SEE YOU AGAIN...
...IF YA EVER MESS WITH MY FAMILY OR MY FRIENDS...
...I'M NOT GONNA BE AS NICE AS I WAS TODAY, AN' I'LL FINISH YER ALABASTER ASS FER GOOD!
NOW, DO YERSELF A FAVOR AND FER ONCE IN YER MISERABLE LIFE SAY NUTHIN'.
NO CHATTIN'...
NO CHORTLIN'...
...JUST LIE THERE AN' BLEED.
KAY, BY, ALL FIN--
?!
gakk

!
WHOMMPP

Uh. WOW. OKAY THEN.
LET'S GET OUTTA HERE. I'VE HAD ENOUGH A' THIS PLACE.

HAAARRLEYYY...
YOU STILL LOVE ME, HARLEY. YOU CAN'T LIVE WITHOUT ME AND IT DRIVES YOU INSANE.
YOU'LL NEVER RID YOURSELF OF ME.
WITHOUT ME, YOU'RE NOTHING.
HEH-HEH.
I FINALLY GET WHY BATMAN NEVER JUST KILLED YOU ALL THESE YEARS.
IT WOULD GIVE YOU EXACTLY WHATCHA WANT.
A-HEH. HEH HEH HEH HEH HEHHH...

YOU HEAR THAT?
A BOAT ENGINE. IVY.
YOU OKAY?
NAW, BUT I'LL BE BETTER.
HURRY, GET IN!
I THINK THE OWNER IS ON TO ME.
Aw, KILLER RIDE!
I'M FEELIN' BETTER ALREADY!
GOTHAM'S SO PRETTY FROM THIS DISTANCE.
YOU MISS IT?
I MISS MY FRIENDS, BUT THE CITY ITSELF HAS CHANGED... I'VE CHANGED, TOO.
I LOVE THE HOME I HAVE NOW.
WELL, GOTHAM CERTAINLY ISN'T THE SAME WITHOUT--
Uh oh, WE HAVE A PROBLEM.
IVY, OF ALL THE BOATS YOU COULD HAVE STOLEN...
WELL, HELLO THERE, BATMAN.
WHAT THE WHAT--? IT'S MY CREW!
MOM!

Seems while we were away, Big Tony an' the gang explained the situation to Batman. I guess Tony's more connected than I thought.
Bats was unusually understandin' about the boat bein' borrowed. He had some thoughts on the whole situation as well, which I was about ta find out.
The Arkham mayhem, we were told, was under control an' there was an all points bulletin put out for Mason's arrest. I have no idea how Batman knows all this. Maybe he's got antennas in those ears?
I'M GOING TO GET YOUR FRIEND MASON IN A WITNESS PROTECTION PROGRAM. HE'S GOING TO HELP GET NEW YORK'S MAYOR OUT OF OFFICE.
TO DO THIS, I NEED YOU TO STAND DOWN AND LET THE AUTHORITIES DO THEIR WORK. AM I MAKING MYSELF CLEAR?
WAIT, BUT I'LL NEVER SEE HIM AGAIN...
YOU WILL, BUT NOT FOR A VERY LONG TIME.
HARLEY, IT'S THE ONLY WAY TO END ALL THIS. BATMAN SAID I COULD CUT A DEAL AND REDUCE MY PRISON TIME BY HELPIN' OUT WITH THE CORRUPTION INVESTIGATION.
THE REALITY IS, SOMEONE DIED BY MY HAND. I GOTTA DO MY TIME FOR THAT, EVEN IF IT WAS AN ACCIDENT.
I WILL BE GOING AS WELL. HARLEY, I NEED YOU TO LOOK AFTER MY BUSINESS WHILE I AM TAKING CARE OF MY BOY.
I...I UNNERSTAND.

I KNOW GOTTA DO THIS, UT IT'S A LOT TO BSORB. I WANT HAT'S BEST FOR OU, BUT I WANT WHAT I WANT, Y'KNOW?
THAT, I UNDERSTAND THE MOST ABOUT YOU, HARLEY. MEETING YOU IS THE BEST THING THAT'S EVER HAPPENED TO ME. I'M NOT GOING TO FORGET WHAT YOU DID FOR MY MOM AND I. RIGHT NOW I GOTTA DO THE RIGHT THING AND CLEAR MY CONSCIENCE.
YEAH, I GET THAT.
SMOOOCH
JEALOUS?
NEVER. I'M HAPPY WHEN SHE'S HAPPY.
BEAUTIFUL AND WISE. WHO WOULDN'T BE ATTRACTED TO THAT?

YOU WILL BE LEAVING GOTHAM. CORRECT?
COOL YER BAT-JETS. I GOT A LIFE AN' A FAMILY THAT NEEDS ME BACK HOME.
GOOD. I'M KEEPING AN EYE ON YOU, QUINZEL.
ONLY OUT AT NIGHT, WEARS ALL BLACK AND A MASK, KEEPS AN EYE ON PRETTY GIRLS.
YUP, YOU MY FRIEND ARE A TEXTBOOK VOYEUR. SEEK SOME HELP.
KEYS.
I OWE YOU ONE.
YES. YOU DO.

NEXT TIME WE GET TOGETHER, LET IT BE FOR A VACATION IN THE BAHAMAS, OKAY?

SUN, SAND, UMBRELLA DRINKS. PROMISE?
I PROMISE.
TRY TO CHEER UP, KIDDO IT'LL ALL B FINE.

A FEW HOURS LATER.
HEY KID, YOU ALL RIGHT?
I WILL BE. TODAY WAS RIDICULOUSLY ROUGH. I FEEL EMOTIONALLY EXHAUSTIFIED.
UNDERSTOOD. THE GOOD NEWS IS, WE'LL ALL BE HOME IN A FEW HOURS.
COME AN' GIVE BIG TONY A HUG. YOU'LL FEEL BETTER.

Aww, YOU'RE RIGHT. I DO FEEL BETTER ALREADY.

WOW. Y'KNOW, NOW WE HAVE A WHOLE WAX MUSEUM TA TAKE CARE OF. THAT'LL BE FUN, RIGHT?
THINGS KEEP CHANGIN', huh?
WE'LL MAKE IT WORK, SOMEHOW. WE ALWAYS DO.
IT'S ONE A' THE FEW THINGS YA CAN DEPEND ON, PEACHE

HEY QUEENIE, HOW ARE YOU AT MAKEOVERS?
I LIVE FOR THE CHALLENGE. ANYTHING IN MIND?

OH, YEAH.
I GOT A WHOLE AVALANCHE OF IDEAS!

HEY! YOU UP THERE!
WE GOT REPORTS THAT YOU SLEEZENHEIMERS HAVE BEEN ILLEGALLY DUMPIN' TRASH INTA THE WATERS AROUND CONEY ISLAND EVERY TIME YOUR TANKER DELIVERS A SHIPMENT-- AN' EVERYONE WANTS IT TA STOP!
DUMP ANY MORE A' YOUR SMELLY-ASS GARBAGE INTA MY OCEAN AN' I SWEAR I'LL GO ALL TITANIC ON YOUR BIG METAL ASS!
BE CAREFUL WHAT YOU WISH FOR
AMANDA CONNER & JIMMY PALMIOTTI writers
AMANDA CONNER artist
CHAD HARDIN artist (pages 8-10)
PAUL MOUNTS colors ALEX SINCLAIR colors (pages 8-10) JOHN J. HILL letters AMANDA CONNER & PAUL MOUNTS cover
DAVE WIELGOSZ asst. editor CHRIS CONROY editor MARK DOYLE group editor HARLEY QUINN created by PAUL DINI & BRUCE TIMM

HEY, LADY, WHAT I DO IS NONE A' YER BUSINESS, SO WHY DON'T YOU *MOVE* THAT *CUTE LITTLE BUTT* OF YOURS *AWAY* SO I CAN DELIVER THIS SHIPMENT?
ELLE POUBELLE
CUTE???

I DON'T THINK IT'S MY *BUTT* YOU SHOULD BE WOR... *whu...*
WHOA!

...WORRIED ABOUT, *CAPTAIN POLLUTION!* ONE PULL A' THIS *TRIGGER...*
...whoops...
...AN' I CAN...
...Whoa NELLY.

YEEOOOWWW!!

BA-BOOOOOM
WHOOPSIE DAISIES!

MAM'SELLE POUBELLE
Bluh-bloh!

YIKES!
I'M GONNA GET SPIN CYCLED!
I'M ALSO GONNA GET SICK!
B-- B--
BLAAAARRRRFF
OH NO! THIS CAN'T BE HOW IT ENDS!
I CAN'T DIE ON AN EMPTY STOMACH!
!
AWESOME!
HOW COOL IS THIS?!
?!

GAAKKK!
-Kaff- -kaff-
POWER GIRL?!
GOOD. YOU'RE BREATHING.
SO, YOU WERE FINE WHEN I SAVED YOU FROM BEING CLOBBERED BY THAT GIANT ANCHOR... WHY DID YOU SWALLOW ALL THAT WATER?
-Mmphh-

I REALLY LIKE MOUTH-TO-MOUTH.
-Sigh-

WELL, YOU'RE LUCKY I WAS NEARBY. ANOTHER FEW SECONDS...
YEAH, I WOULDA GOTTEN TA BE A GHOST AN' HAUNT EVERYONE.
YOU KNOW, SEE WHAT THEY DO IN THOSE QUIET MOMENTS...
WELL, I'M GLAD I WAS ABLE TO RESCUE YOU AND THE CREW OF THAT SHIP.
WHAT EXACTLY WERE YOU TRYING TO DO? BETTER YET, DON'T TELL ME. I HAVE TO RUN.

NOT WITHOUT A HUG. THANK YOU SOOO MUCH.
AN' REMEMBER, YOU NEED ME TA PLAY SIDEKICK AGAIN, YOU JUST HOLLER AN' I'M READY.
UH, YEAH. SURE.

OKAY, MY LI'L SEA TREASURE...
LET'S SEE IF YA GOT ANY INTERESTIN' MESSAGES IN YOU.

UGGHNNNN!
UGGHHHNNN!
COME ON, GET OFF, WILL YA?

UGHHHHH... COME ON!

HA!
POIP

GREAT, I JUST UNLEASHED A TOXIC GAS UPON THE WORLD.
PEE-YEW, IT SMELLS LIKE ANCIENT FARTS.

WHO HAS AWAKENED THE GREAT JIMM SALABIM?
!?
MY MISTRESS, YOU HAVE RELEASED ME FROM THE PRISON OF THE BOTTLE.
I AM HERE FOR YOU TO COMMAND, AND TO GRANT YOU ALL YOUR WISHES.
SERIOUS? YOU'RE A REAL GENIE?
ONE OF THREE IN THE KNOWN UNIVERSE. HOW MAY I PLEASE YOU?
SLOWLY AN' WITH GREAT PASSION, BUT OTHER THAN THAT, HOW MANY WISHES DO I GET?

AS MANY AS YOU ASK. SAY THE WORDS AND I WILL SHOW YOU MY POWER.
SO, IF I SAY I WISH I HAD A DOZEN SHISH KEBABS, YOU WOULD GET 'EM FOR ME?
YOUR WISH IS MY COMMAND.

KASTAN-BLAA

BEHOLD, MY MISTRESS. SHISH KEBABS.
EEEEEEE!

IT HAS BEEN AGES SINCE I HAVE DINED. THANK YOU FOR SHARING YOUR BOUNTY, MISTRESS.
IT WILL BE A PLEASURE GRANTING YOUR DESIRES.
OH, YEAH? Y'KNOW WHAT I REALLY DESIRE?
SAY THE WORD, MISTRESS.
DIDJA SEE THE GIRL THAT PULLED US OUTTA THE WATER?
Ahh... THE GOLDEN-HAIRED, TALL ONE BLESSED WITH THE BOUNTIFUL SHAMMAMS.
YEAH, THAT ONE. WELL, I WANT SHAMMAMS JUST LIKE HERS!
YOU DESIRE SUCH PLENITUDE?
SO BE IT.
KASTANBLAA

HOLEE HEAPIN' HONEYDEWS--
Wh... whu... whoa--!
POOOMF!

FRANKIE BAGS!
OKAY, NOT LIKE I IMAGINED.
I CHANGED MY MIND. I WISH THEY WERE GONE... NO, WAIT, WAIT--!
I WISH THEY WERE BACK TO MY ORIGINAL SIZE. AN' THEN TAKE US HOME.
AN' WHILE YER AT IT, CAN YA GET THE SAND OUTTA THIS CAVERNOUS CASABA CRACK?
YOUR WISH IS GRANTED, MY MISTRESS.
KASTAN BLAA

Ahh...THAT'S BETTER!
WHAT AN INTERESTING ABODE.
Madame Macabre's
HEY, FRUITCAKES, YOU KNOW HOW THIS ENDS, DON'T YA? HOW MANY TIMES HAVE YA HEARD THIS STORY?
THIS IS DIFFERENT, BERNIE. I KNOW WHAT I'M DOING.
THAT SENTENCE ALONE IS ENOUGH TO MAKE ME LEAVE TOWN, IF ONLY MY LEGS WORKED.
IT REMINDS ME OF THE SCRUMPOX STYES OF SUBARTU.
JIM SALMON BIB, I WISH MY BEAVER WAS MORE ENERGETIC AN' LIVELY.
Er, IT IS JIMM SALABIM, MISTRESS.
AND DO YOU MEAN "ALIVE"?
SURE!
IT IS DONE.
KASTANBLAA
!
SQUEEEEEE
WAIT, HE WAS ALIVE, AN' NOW HE'S DEAD? WHY?
IT MAY BE THE GIANT HOLE AND THE BESCORCHED HIDE IS THE CULPRIT?
OH. YEAH.
Hmmm, I NEED TA BE SMARTER HERE. SOMETHING MORE INTEREST...
A-HA!
OKAY, TIM BADA BIM, HERE'S A CHALLENGE.
I WISH THE JOKER WAS A NICER, MORE SENSITIVE GUY AN' WE WERE STILL DATING.
YOUR DESIRES ARE MY PASSION, MISTRESS.
KASTANBLAA

YOU'RE NEXT, COMMISSIONER GORDON.
CRAP.
I HATE THESE CHECK UPS.
IF THE JOB DIDN'T MAKE ME DO THIS, I PROBABLY WOULDN'T COME AT ALL.
COME NOW, COMMISSIONER. WHAT IN THIS MISERABLE WORLD IS MORE BEAUTIFUL...

...THAN A NICE BIG, HANDSOME SMILE?
THE LOVE OF ONE'S MOTHER?
THAT'S SO TRUE. I NEVER THOUGHT OF THAT. I DO MISS HER.

WAIT A MINUTE! WHAT'S GOIN' ON HERE?
THIS ISN'T RIGHT.
GORDON'S SUPPOSED TA BE TIED TO THE CHAIR, WITH YOU READY TO DRILL ALL HIS TEETH OUT!

NOW, CUPCAKE, A SMILE IS SERIOUS BUSINESS. MOTHER TERESA SAID IT BEST: PEACE BEGINS WITH A SMILE.
SHE WAS A WISE WOMAN.
AND A HUMANITARIAN. DID YOU KNOW SHE WON THE NOBEL PEACE PRIZE IN 1978?
IS THAT A FACT?
NO! I DON'T LIKE THIS AT ALL! YOU'RE TOO NICE!
HI, AM I TOO EARLY FOR MY APPOINTMENT?
WHAT NOW?

BATMAN, I'M RUNNING A BIT LATE.
I'LL FINISH WITH THE COMMISSIONER, THEN WE CAN TACKLE THAT TOOTH THAT'S BEEN BOTHERING YOU.
THANKS, DOC. IT HURT SO BAD, I TOOK IT OUT ON THE PENGUIN'S FACE.
HE LOOKED LIKE THE BUSINESS END OF A TURKEY DINNER BY THE TIME I WAS DONE.
I DO THAT ALL THE TIME. FEELS GOOD TO BEAT A PERP WITH THE BUTT OF MY PISTOL NOW AND AGAIN...
...AND IT'S GREAT EXERCISE!
YOU TWO CRACK ME UP! NO NEED TO PUT ON A SHOW, I KNOW YOU'RE ONLY SAYING THAT STUFF TO MAKE ME LAUGH. AND IT WORKED...
HAHAHA HAHAHAHA
TER...
I FEEL PRETTY... OH, SO PRETTY...
A-hem.
A-hemmm!
DARLING, I AM SO SORRY.
I WAS SO WRAPPED UP IN MY WORK, I...WELL, I APOLOGIZE.
JUST LOOK AT YOU! THAT NEW NIGHTIE IS AMAZING. YOU LOOK SO BEAUTIFUL, I JUST WANNA CRY!
WOW! THANKS!
NO, I REALLY WANNA CRY.

WAAAAAAA!
SNIFF. POOPSIE... YOU'RE SO... SO LOVELY...
WAAAAAAA!
HEY! GET A GRIP ALREADY!
TURN OFF THE FLOODGATES AN' TURN ON THE CHARM!
WAAAAAAA!!!
I'M TRYING, POOPSIE, THEN I START THINKING ABOUT... SNIFF... THE CHILDREN!
WAAAAAAA!!!
OW-OW-OW-OW.
OW-OW-OW-OW.
THE CHILDREN.
Sigh
OW-OW-OW-OW-OW.
PUNT
AN' STOP CALLIN' ME POOPSIE!
SLAM
GIN CHALLA RIM, I WISH THIS WHOLE PATHETIC SITUATION AWAY, AN' I WANNA BE HOME!

WELL THAT WAS A DISASTER. LET'S TRY SOMETHIN' DIFFERENT.
YARF!
WAIT, I THINK I GOT IT!
I WISH I COULD UNDERSTAN' AN' COMMUNICATE WITH ALL LIVIN' CREATURES.
THAT IS A GOOD WISH, MY MISTRESS.
WHY, THANK YOU. MAKE IT HAPPEN, JIMBO.
IT SHALL BE SO.
KASTANBLAM

...

SO THAT'S IT?
YEAH, I DIDN'T SEE NOTHIN'.
RIGHT?

WHITHMINIT...
NATHAN, YOU CAN TALK!

AND YOU CAN UNDERSTAND ME. GOOD.
I GOT SOMETHING I NEED TO GET OFF MY DOGGIE CHEST.
SPEAK AWAY, MY FUZZY FRIEND.

LOOK, I LOVE HE SCRATCHING ND PETTING AND BELLY RUBS, BUT YOU GOTTA GET ME A GIRLFRIEND ALREADY.
I GOT NEEDS LIKE EVERYONE ELSE.
OH, AND THE FARTING IN YOUR SLEEP HAS GOT TO STOP.
I LIKE TO GET IN THE VICINITY OF THAT SPOT FOR THE WARMTH, BUT HOLY BEAN SUPREME, GIRL!

I SWEAR I LOSE A PATCH OF FUR EVERY TIME YOU BLAST THE MORNING WAKE-UP WHISTLE.
OH-MY-GOD!

AND THAT BEAVER OF YOURS...YOU GOTTA GIVE IT A REST.
WHY, I NEVER!
YOU TALK TO IT LIKE IT'S ALIVE, AND IT'S A BIT WEIRD IF YOU ASK ME.
OH, AND THE NERVE OF YOU EATING PIZZA, AND THEN YOU FEED ME MOOSE PARTS OUT OF A CAN.
DID I DO SOMETHING TO TICK YOU OFF?
BLOOD.

WHAT? DID YOU JUST SAY BLOOD?
BLOOD!

TASTY BLOOD. EAT IT UP!
NO, YOU DON'T!
YEAH, I DO.
LISTEN, YOU GOT ABOUT A BILLION GALLONS IN YOU, AND EVEN IF I TAKE A LITTLE, YOU MAKE MORE, SO WHAT'S THE PROBLEM?
IT'S MY BLOOD!

WHERE ARE YOU HIDING, YOU PLASMA SWILLIN' PEST?!

RIGHT HERE, NUTCASE!

BOOOM

SORRY 'BOUT THAT, TIM BADA BIM.
WORRY NOT, MISTRESS. ONE CANNOT HARM GENIES WITH WEAPONS, ONLY WORDS.
DO YOU WISH THE PEST TO BEGONE?
NO THANKS. I GOT THIS.

GET BACK HERE, YA BUZZY LI'L BASTARD!
ZZZZZZZZZZZZ

ZZZZZZZZZZZIP!

THAT'S IT! YOU ARE DEAD MEAT!

Eeep!

OHMIGOD!
NONO NO! COME BACK!
I DIDN'T MEAN YOU GUYS!
MAMA WOULD NEVER HURT HER BABIES!
WE'RE GONNA DIE!
RUN FOR YOUR LIVES!
IT'S ALL OVER!

Mmm Yummm.
WHAT'S THAT?
YOU SMELL WAY BETTER THAN THAT POOP I WAS JUST EATING.
CAN I LICK YOU?
FERGET IT, PAL! SHE WON'T EVEN LET YA TASTE HER!

AAAAAHHH!!!
UN-WISH! UN-WISH!
CONSIDER IT DONE.
KASTAN-BLAAA

I REALLY SUCK AT THIS, DON'T I?
WELL, THE LAST MASTER I HAD SAID HE WANTED TO BE KING OF THE MOON. SHALL WE SAY YOU'RE DOING QUITE BETTER THAN HE.
YOU GAVE HIM A SPACE SUIT, RIGHT?
I HAVE NO IDEA WHAT THAT IS. LAST TIME I WAS OUT OF MY BOTTLE WAS IN HABSBURG, SPAIN, THE YEAR 1518.
FLOOR MODEL DO NOT REMOVE
LIK-RISH LASSOS
POP CORN
Whoa.
OKAY, I'M GONNA BE SPECIFIC WITH THIS ONE.
I WISH I WAS WONDER WOMAN!
CLASSIC WARRIOR ON HORSEBACK?
70'S WHITE SLACKS ONE?
PEREZ-CRISIS?
TV ONE?
LUNCH-PAIL WONDER WOMAN?
CLIFF CHIANG NEW 52 ONE?
FORGET IT. I PASS.
WAIT A MINUTE, SO HOW D'YA KNOW STUFF LIKE THE DIFFERENT WONDER WOMANS AN' WHO THE JOKER IS AN' ALL THAT IF YOU HAVEN'T BEEN OUT A' YER BOTTLE PRISON SINCE THEN?
GENIE POWERS. I KNOW NOT HOW IT WORKS, BUT I'M ABLE TO TURN TO SMOKE, GRANT WISHES AND MANY OTHER ENSORCELMENTS.
IF I MAY ASK, HOW ARE ALL THOSE PEOPLE IN THE LITTLE BOX WE ARE WATCHING?
NEVER MIND. I G ANOTHE WISH...
I WISH TO INVISIBL
IT SHALL BE.
KASTAN-BLAA
WOW! THIS IS INCREDIBLE!
NOW FER PART TWO A' THE WISH.
I WANNA BE IN JUSTICE LEAGUE HEADQUARTERS FER THEIR ANNUAL SUPERHERO MEETIN'.
THIS, TOO, SHALL BE.
KASTANBLA

HOLY CRAP!
I CAN SEE MY HOUSE FROM HERE!

THIS THREAT IS LIKE NOTHING WE HAVE EVER ENCOUNTERED AND IT'S HEADING TOWARDS EARTH RIGHT NOW!
OH, THIS IS GONNA BE FUN!

GREAT HAMMER OF HEPHAESTUS!
FOOOOMP

Huh... I HAVE NO IDEA HOW THAT HAPPENED.
MAYBE THE ELASTIC IS WORN?
A GRAVITATIONAL ANOMALY, PERHAPS?
Hmmmm...

WHAT'S WRONG?
HEY!
THWAP

LIKE YOU DON'T KNOW.

HA HAHA HAHA!
WHAT THE--!
SNORT

SEEMS LIKE WE HAVE AN INVISIBLE VISITOR CAUSING A BIT OF CHAOS.
RUNNING OVER EVERY SINGLE INCH OF THE FLOOR AT SUPER SPEED OUGHTA PINPOINT THE CULPRIT.

INCOMING!
Whoa!
Trip
SORRY, BATS.
I GOT THIS.
HEY! OKAY, THIS IS ENOUGH.
OOOF!
WHAPP
OWWWW!
DANGER
RE-ENTRY PROGRAM LAUNCH TRIGGER
KUNK
WASTE
WHATZ'IS?
DANGER
RE-ENTRY PROGRAM LAUNCH TRIGGER
BOOMP
AAAAAHHH!!!
JIMM-UNDOTHEWISH-AN'GETME-HOMEQUICK!
KASTANBLAA

Whew! HOLEE CRAP, THAT WAS CLOSE!
OH! HEY, GUYS!
BEHOLD! I CAN MAKE HER APPEAR.
WHOA, SO YOU ARE A REAL GENIE!
AMAZING! CAN WE GET WISHES, TOO?
ONLY MY MISTRESS CAN COMMAND ME TO GRANT A WISH.

HEY, PEACHES, DO ME A FAVOR AN' ASK HIM FER A MILLION BUCKS. BETWEEN THIS PLACE, THE BILLS AN' EVERYTHING, WE CAN SURE USE THE CASH.
SMEK
OF COURSE! WHY DIDN'T I THINK A' THAT?

JING BADA BING, I WOULD LIKE A MILLION BUCKS!
ASK, AND YOU SHALL RECEIVE.

KASTAN BLAA
Uh oh, WAIT--

JIMBO... IF YOU COULD...
GRANTED.

KASTAN BLAA
GUYS, DO ME A FAVOR AN' LEAVE ME WITH MY GENIE BUDDY FER A FEW. I GOT A COUPLE A' THINGS TA WORK OUT.
OKAY, BUT DON'T WEAR HIM DOWN. WE CAN REALLY USE THIS GUY.

FOR YOUR INFORMATION, I DO NOT "WEAR DOWN".
YOU, MY FINE SIR, HAVE NO IDEA WHAT YOU ARE DEALING WITH.

OKAY, I THOUGHT OF A BUNCH MORE WISHES. YOU READY?
AS YOU WISH, MY MIS--
YEAH, YEAH, HERE WE GO.

NOW CAN I WISH FOR A NEW ROOF?
DAFFODILL
AAAAHHH!!! NOOO!
THAT'S NOT WHAT I MEANT! MAKE IT STOP NOW!
YI
YIYIYI
YI
NO. NO. NO. NOT THIS KIND OF STAR!
THIS WAS SO MUCH BETTER IN MY HEAD.
I SAID "PENTAGON"!!!
-Sigh-
I DON'T SEE WHAT THE BIG FREAKIN' DEAL IS.
AN' WHY IS THERE SO MUCH POOP UP HERE?

I'VE HAD ENOUGH A' THIS!
EVERY SINGLE THING I ASK FOR GOES WRONG AND TURNS INTO A BIG, FAT, GIANT DISASTER!
BUT, MY MISTRESS... I ONLY DO AS YOU COMMAND.

YEAH, AN' SOMEHOW I END UP PAYIN' FER IT!
BUT--
HEY, JIN SALAD LIMB, Y'KNOW WHAT I WISH!?
I WISH YOU DIDN'T HAVE THESE STUPID POWERS!
BUT--

VERY WELL.
KASTAN-BLAA.

WHY DIDJA FALL D-- OH NO!
I DIDN'T MEAN THAT! I WISH YOU HAD YOUR POWERS BACK!
IT IS TOO LATE. YOU WISHED IT, AND ACCORDING TO THE RULES, I GAVE IT TO YOU.
BUT... DON'T I GET A DO-OVER? MAYBE A RETRO-WISH?
SADLY, YOU NOT ONLY STRIPPED ME OF MY POWERS, BUT I AM A MORTAL NOW.

WAIT A MINUTE, THOSE GENIE POWERS... THEY...
RENDERED ME IMMORTAL, AMONG OTHER THINGS.
I AM NOW CONFINED, LIKE YOU, IN THIS FLESHY SHELL 'TIL I DIE A NATURAL, OR UNNATURAL, DEATH.
IS IT ME, OR IS IT COLD IN HERE?

I HAVE NO CLOTHING. I HAVE... NOTHING.
NO HOME... NO FRIENDS...
AW, SWEETIE, NONONO, PLEASE DON'T FEEL BAD. YER GONNA MAKE ME CRY.
FOR THE FIRST TIME IN MY LIFE, I AM TRULY ALONE.
YOU CAN STAY WITH ME, AND YA GOT ALL THE FRIENDS YOU WANT.
HERE. PUT THIS ON.

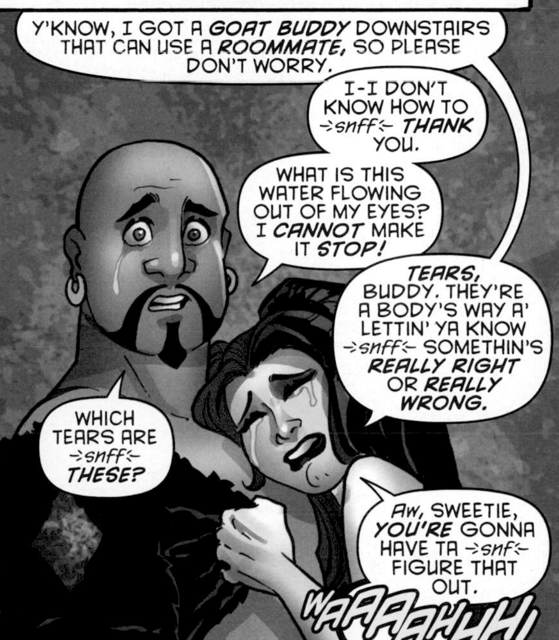
Y'KNOW, I GOT A GOAT BUDDY DOWNSTAIRS THAT CAN USE A ROOMMATE, SO PLEASE DON'T WORRY.
I-I DON'T KNOW HOW TO -snff- THANK YOU.
WHAT IS THIS WATER FLOWING OUT OF MY EYES? I CANNOT MAKE IT STOP!
TEARS, BUDDY. THEY'RE A BODY'S WAY A' LETTIN' YA KNOW -snff- SOMETHIN'S REALLY RIGHT OR REALLY WRONG.
WHICH TEARS ARE -snff- THESE?
AW, SWEETIE, YOU'RE GONNA HAVE TA -snf- FIGURE THAT OUT.
WAAAAHHH!

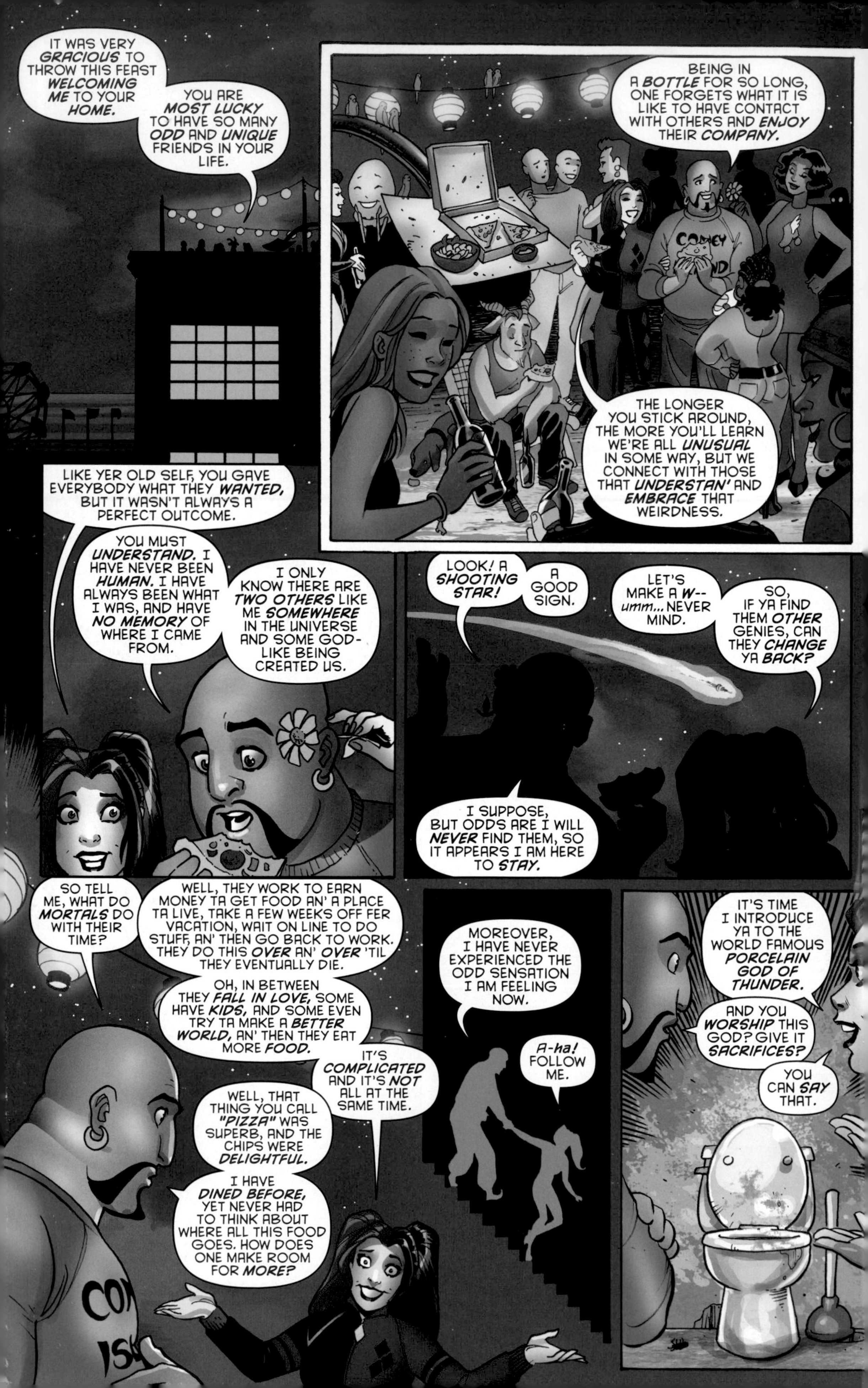
IT WAS VERY GRACIOUS TO THROW THIS FEAST WELCOMING ME TO YOUR HOME.
YOU ARE MOST LUCKY TO HAVE SO MANY ODD AND UNIQUE FRIENDS IN YOUR LIFE.
BEING IN A BOTTLE FOR SO LONG, ONE FORGETS WHAT IT IS LIKE TO HAVE CONTACT WITH OTHERS AND ENJOY THEIR COMPANY.
THE LONGER YOU STICK AROUND, THE MORE YOU'LL LEARN WE'RE ALL UNUSUAL IN SOME WAY, BUT WE CONNECT WITH THOSE THAT UNDERSTAN' AND EMBRACE THAT WEIRDNESS.
LIKE YER OLD SELF, YOU GAVE EVERYBODY WHAT THEY WANTED, BUT IT WASN'T ALWAYS A PERFECT OUTCOME.
YOU MUST UNDERSTAND. I HAVE NEVER BEEN HUMAN. I HAVE ALWAYS BEEN WHAT I WAS, AND HAVE NO MEMORY OF WHERE I CAME FROM.
I ONLY KNOW THERE ARE TWO OTHERS LIKE ME SOMEWHERE IN THE UNIVERSE AND SOME GOD-LIKE BEING CREATED US.
LOOK! A SHOOTING STAR!
A GOOD SIGN.
LET'S MAKE A W-- umm... NEVER MIND.
SO, IF YA FIND THEM OTHER GENIES, CAN THEY CHANGE YA BACK?
I SUPPOSE, BUT ODDS ARE I WILL NEVER FIND THEM, SO IT APPEARS I AM HERE TO STAY.
SO TELL ME, WHAT DO MORTALS DO WITH THEIR TIME?
WELL, THEY WORK TO EARN MONEY TA GET FOOD AN' A PLACE TA LIVE, TAKE A FEW WEEKS OFF FER VACATION, WAIT ON LINE TO DO STUFF, AN' THEN GO BACK TO WORK. THEY DO THIS OVER AN' OVER 'TIL THEY EVENTUALLY DIE.
OH, IN BETWEEN THEY FALL IN LOVE, SOME HAVE KIDS, AND SOME EVEN TRY TA MAKE A BETTER WORLD, AN' THEN THEY EAT MORE FOOD.
IT'S COMPLICATED AND IT'S NOT ALL AT THE SAME TIME.
WELL, THAT THING YOU CALL "PIZZA" WAS SUPERB, AND THE CHIPS WERE DELIGHTFUL.
I HAVE DINED BEFORE, YET NEVER HAD TO THINK ABOUT WHERE ALL THIS FOOD GOES. HOW DOES ONE MAKE ROOM FOR MORE?
MOREOVER, I HAVE NEVER EXPERIENCED THE ODD SENSATION I AM FEELING NOW.
A-ha! FOLLOW ME.
IT'S TIME I INTRODUCE YA TO THE WORLD FAMOUS PORCELAIN GOD OF THUNDER.
AND YOU WORSHIP THIS GOD? GIVE IT SACRIFICES?
YOU CAN SAY THAT.